PISTOL PACKIN' MADAMS

TRUE STORIES OF NOTORIOUS WOMEN OF THE OLD WEST

CHRIS ENSS

TWODOT®

GUILFORD, CONNECTICUT
HELENA, MONTANA
AN IMPRINT OF THE GLOBE PEQUOT PRESS

A · T W O D O T® · B O O K

Copyright © 2006 by Chris Enss

Text design by Lisa Reneson

Library of Congress Cataloging-in-Publication Data
Enss, Chris, 1961-
   Pistol packin' madams : true stories of notorious women of the Old West / Chris Enss.— 1st ed.
       p. cm.
   Includes bibliographical references.
   ISBN-13: 978-0-7627-3775-8
   ISBN-10: 0-7627-3775-1
   1. Prostitution—West (U.S.)—History. 2. Brothels—West (U.S.)—History. 3. Businesswomen—West (U.S.)—History. I. Title: Pistol packing madams. II. Title.
   HQ145.W47E57 2006
   306.74'2092278—dc22

                                                                    2006002618

Manufactured in the United States of America
First Edition/First Printing

For Big Nose Kate, who gave as good as she got from Doc Holliday

CONTENTS

Acknowledgments, ix

Introduction, xi

JENNIE ROGERS: *Queen of the Denver Row*, 1

ELEANORA DUMONT: *Gold Country Angel of Sin*, 9

MADAM HARRIET: *A Curious Criminal Case*, 17

JESSIE HAYMAN: *The San Francisco Favorite*, 21

JESSIE REEVES AND CAD THOMPSON: *Scarlet Ladies in Texas and Nevada*, 29

JOSIE WASHBURN: *Nebraska's Reluctant Madam*, 41

KATE HORONY: *The Hungarian Madam*, 49

MATTIE SILKS: *Denver's Red Light Queen*, 55

FLORENCE MABEL DEDRICK: *Our Sister of the Street*, 61

TESSIE WALL: *Barbary Coast Madam*, 65

LIBBY THOMPSON: *Dodge City's Squirrel Tooth Alice*, 77

ROSE ELLIS: *Last of the Old West Madams*, 83

Bibliography, 89

About the Author, 95

ACKNOWLEDGMENTS

Chasing down the history of the women behind the soiled doves of America's Old West has been a daunting, but rewarding, task. Many organizations contributed to this book and deserve to be recognized.

The Kansas and Colorado Historical Societies kindly provided information about madams Squirrel Tooth Alice, Mattie Silks, and Jennie Rogers.

The San Francisco Public Library offered newspaper clippings and biographical sketches of Tessie Wall and Jessie Hayman.

The Nevada County Historical Library and Searls Library helped locate records on Eleanora Dumont and Texas Tommy. The staff at each of these locations was generous with their time and extremely patient. Their assistance is greatly appreciated.

Thanks also to my brilliant editor, Erin Turner, and the encouraging promotions and sales staff at Globe Pequot Press, in particular Christopher Coates.

INTRODUCTION

If every man was as true to his country as he is to his wife—God help the USA.
—Needlepoint in the main receiving
room of a San Francisco Brothel, 1891

In the mid-1800s, fortune hunters rushed to the western frontier, seeking gold and land. They were quickly joined by merchants, gamblers, and prostitutes—all of them hoping to capitalize on the needs and desires of the intrepid pioneer.

Although some frontier women were able to make a living as laundresses, cooks, and homesteaders, job opportunities for women in the early days of the American West were, by and large, severely limited. It didn't take long for some women to realize the profit to be made by supplying sexual favors to lonely pioneers, miners, and trappers.

According to records at the California State Historical Library, more than half of the working women in the West during the 1870s were prostitutes. At that time, madams—those women who owned, managed, and maintained brothels—were generally the only women out west who appeared to be in control of their own destinies. For that reason alone, the prospect of a career in "the oldest profession"—at least at the outset—must have seemed promising.

Often referred to as "sporting women" and "soiled doves," prostitutes mostly ranged in age from seventeen to twenty-five, although girls as young as fourteen were sometimes hired. Women over twenty-eight years of age were generally considered too old to be prostitutes.

Rarely, if ever, did working women use their real names. In order to avoid trouble with the law as they traveled from town to town, and to protect their true identities, many of these women adopted colorful new handles, like Contrary Mary, Little Gold Dollar, Lazy Kate, and Honolulu Nell. The vicinities where their businesses were located were also given distinctive names. Bordellos and parlor houses typically thrived in that part of the city known as "the half world," "the badlands," "the tenderloin," "the twilight zone," or "the red-light district."

Interestingly, the term "red-light district" originated in Kansas. As a way of discouraging would-be intruders, brazen railroad workers around Dodge City began hanging their red brakemen's lanterns outside their doors as a signal that they were in the company of a lady of the evening. The colorful custom was quickly adopted by many ladies and their madams.

Generally speaking, a prostitute's class was determined by her location and her clientele. High-priced prostitutes plied their trade in parlor houses. These immense, beautiful homes were well furnished and lavishly decorated. The women who worked at such posh houses were impeccably dressed, pampered by personal maids, and protected by the ambitious madams who managed the business. In general, parlor houses were very profitable. Madams kept repeat customers interested by importing women from France, Russia, England, and the East Coast of the United States. These ladies could earn more than $25 a night. The madams received a substantial portion of the proceeds, which were often used to improve the parlor house or to purchase similar houses.

The lifestyle was, without a doubt, a dangerous one, and many women despised being a part of the underworld profession. As madam and prostitute Josie Washburn noted in 1896:

> We are there because we must have bread. The man is there because he must have pleasure; he has no other necessity for being there; true if we were not there the men would not come. But we are not permitted to be anywhere else.

Entertaining numerous men often resulted in assault, unwanted pregnancies, venereal disease, and even death. Some prostitutes escaped the hell of the trade by committing suicide. Some drank themselves to death; others overdosed on laudanum. Botched abortions, syphilis, and other diseases claimed many of their lives as well.

In the late 1860s, a concern for the physical condition of prostitutes—and moreover, for the effect their poor health was having on the community at large—was finally addressed. Government officials, alerted to the spread of infectious illnesses, decided to take action against women of ill repute. At a public meeting in New York City, a bill was introduced that was aimed at curtailing the activities of prostitutes who did not pass health exams. The goal of the bill was to stop the advance of what morally upright citizens termed the "social evil."

A March 14, 1867, *New York Times* article reported on the proceedings:

> The committee on public health today reported Mr. Jacob's bill for further suppression of prostitution. It was amended, at the suggestion of the author, by providing for the medical inspection of all females in registered houses, and the detention of those diseased in a retreat, under the control of the Board of Health.
>
> During the morning large numbers of persons representing the houses of ill fame congregated in the cloak room, bitterly opposing the bill and attempting to smother it. But Dr. Crandall and his associates on the committee stood firm and reported the bill. It will be pushed forward at the earliest possible moment. It provides a heavy penalty upon all persons who let and keep houses for unlawful purposes, of the description named, the penalties being a lien upon the property. The Police Commissioners are directed to cause a registration to be made of all houses of prostitution, and of the inmates in them. The Board of Health are directed to make thorough periodical sanitary

inspections of the registered places, and to remove all diseased persons in them to a "retreat," which they are directed to provide.

The bill receives the endorsement of both the Police and Health authorities. Another bill has been introduced and is now before the committee on state charitable institutions, which proposes to license the houses, and appoint a commission for that purpose. This measure, it is understood, is backed by the parties interested in the business of prostitution, and is not likely to be favorably considered.

As time went on, houses of ill repute and the prostitutes who worked in them came under constant attack from outraged citizens, who insisted the brothels be shut down. Madams hired police to protect their girls and their businesses from forced closures by private citizens. Having such safety measures in place cost madams an initiation fee of $300 to $500. The monthly payment for continued support was $30 to $50. Additionally, expensive fines—ranging from $750 to $900 an offense—were levied against madams who operated houses without a license.

Although prostitution was far from being socially acceptable, it was viewed by many as a necessary evil. The profession was tolerated for two important reasons. First, the public believed that it prevented randy cowboys and miners from raping decent women. Second, given that new mothers were expected to refrain from having sex while breastfeeding—and that children were not completely weaned until they were two years old—it was commonly accepted that husbands in such situations often sought satisfaction in the arms of the ladies of easy virtue.

Still, prostitutes and madams were criticized and looked down upon by "God-fearing" men and women who were infiltrating the West in ever-increasing numbers. A few brave souls dared to defend the "fallen angels," chastising those who passed judgment on them. Some even had poems published in local newspapers, expressing their thoughts on the matter. One such defender was miner John Brantingham, whose verses appeared in a 1901 Colorado newspaper. His words expressed the feelings of many citizens who benefited from the benevolence of the women of ill fame:

> There is so much bad in the best of us.
> And so much good in the worst of us.
> That it hardly behooves any of us
> To talk about the rest of us.

Despite the moral objections to prostitution, madams and their entourages were often greeted with shouts of joy when they first arrived in mining camps. Their presence in the sparsely populated West was cause for celebration among many pioneer men. "Public women" performed a variety of services for lonely men, and in the absence of the men's wives, they offered much-needed comfort and companionship. It was not unusual for these shady ladies to be treated as friends and confidants by their customers.

The fallen women included in this volume learned to live with the negative social stigma associated with their trade. They survived the rough, lawless men in their company and the gossip of "God-fearing" women, and strongly defended themselves whenever the occasion arose.

Nebraska Madam Josie Washburn chose to stand up to critics of her profession in a series of published articles. She blasted the hypocrisy of politicians who sought to eliminate prostitution while continuing to patronize parlor houses. Dodge City's Squirrel Tooth Alice used a revolver instead of a pen to ward off violent, hotheaded patrons. Madam Rose of Nevada City, California, was always armed, but decided to battle the residents who thought she was evil incarnate by giving generously to the poor in the community.

The picture of the early American West would not be complete without the image of a fashionably dressed madam standing at the top of saloon stairs and surveying the activity below. All eyes watched as she stepped down into her domain to make sure the women in her care were showing clients a good time. *Pistol Packin' Madams* examines the stories of these resourceful but much-maligned women, whose combined adventures offer a colorful and often-overlooked portrait of the early days of the West.

JENNIE ROGERS

QUEEN OF THE DENVER ROW

*Each afternoon about three o'clock, the august
lawmakers would retire to Jennie Rogers's Palace of Joy
on Market Street and there disport themselves in riotous
fashion.*
　　　　　　　　　　—*The Rocky Mountain News,* 1890

A blood orange sun shone down on the dusty main thoroughfare in
Denver, Colorado. Miners and townspeople hurried about their daily
activities, pausing every so often to talk with friends and acquaintances.
A sudden commotion at the end of the street drew attention away from
their regular routines. An open, horse-drawn coach, carrying a host of
overly painted girls, had rolled into the bustling mining town. The
bawdy cargo drew stares and disapproving gasps from the town's
respectable women.

Jennie Rogers, a tall, attractive madam and self-proclaimed
"Queen of the Colorado Underworld," steered the rig slowly past the
shops and saloons. The raven-haired woman was dressed in a green velvet dress and was wearing a beautiful pair of emerald earrings. The other
fancily dressed ladies in the coach waved at the gathering crowd that
lined the streets. Cowpunchers, miners, and outlaws shouted out their
approval as they eyed the stunning parade of females.

The prostitutes' low-cut bodices showed enough of their youth-
fully solid and well-rounded necks and breasts to entice the onlookers.
It was exactly the kind of response Jennie had hoped to provoke.

Amorous men followed the coach to a parlor house on Market Street, and there, history records, "a good time was had by all."

Denver's red-light district was a busy area. Prospectors had invaded the town some thirty years earlier, and the discovery of gold had sparked an influx of miners and their families. By the time Jennie Rogers arrived on the scene in 1879, the gold camp had become a booming city with a network of railroads and a variety of profitable industries in place. Madams converged on the growing Colorado territory to amass their own fortunes, offering a service that many lonely men considered a necessary evil.

Madam Rogers's two-story brick brothel was a popular stop for those living in or passing through the region. It was furnished with enamel and brass beds, along with hand-carved dressers, desks, and chairs. Lace curtains and imported rugs rounded out the interior decor. The house was a lavish oasis for its rough guests, and was precisely the type of establishment Jennie had envisioned owning when she got into the business in her twenties.

Born in Allegheny, Pennsylvania, on the Fourth of July in 1843, Jennie was originally named Leah. Her father, James Weaver, was a poor farmer. When she was old enough, Jennie helped make ends meet by selling the family's homegrown produce in the street markets of Pittsburgh. Her natural good looks prompted many men to propose marriage. However, it wasn't until Doctor G. Friess, a prominent physician in the area, asked for her hand that Jennie agreed to marry.

Doctor Friess's practice kept him away from home quite often, and his very sociable wife was frequently left alone. In a short time Jennie tired of the solitary lifestyle and left the marriage.

Yearning for adventure, she took off with a captain of a steamship and traveled the waterways between Pennsylvania and Ohio. After several years, however, life on the river lost its luster. She abandoned the relationship in favor of working as a housekeeper on dry land.

In the mid-1870s, Jennie took a position as a domestic at the home of the mayor of Pittsburgh. While there, she spoke openly about her previous affairs, and the news that she had left two men eventually reached the public at large. The mayor's constituency was outraged that he would allow a woman with such questionable morals to work in his house. As a result, the mayor let her go, but not before advancing her a substantial amount of money to back a business she wanted to start in St. Louis, Missouri.

Historians have no idea why Jennie chose to pursue a career as a madam. She was an astute businesswoman and must have intuitively known the money to be made in arranging company for lonely men. Whatever the reason, her first parlor house in St. Louis was a huge success. Many laborers and business magnates flocked to her "fashionable resort."

When news of a gold strike in Colorado reached Jennie, she decided to travel west to the Mile High City and consider opening a second parlor house there. After seeing the flood of humanity that had descended upon Denver, and calculating how much money there was to be made, she decided to purchase another brothel. Jennie paid $4,600 for the house, and in less than a month, she had made back her investment.

Jennie's Denver business was located in a section of town known as "The Row." Similar houses stood next to hers and were run by some of the most famous madams of the time. Mattie Silks, Laura Evans, and Lizzie Preston all had successful businesses in the same location.

Not everyone appreciated the services Jennie and the other women had to offer. Respectable citizens demanded the city council take action against the numerous "dens of iniquity." In an effort to shame the madams into shutting their houses down, the council ordered all "women of ill repute" to wear yellow ribbons. Undaunted by the attempt to humiliate them, Jennie and the other madams decided to dress in yellow from head to toe. Their dresses, shoes, and parasols were yellow, and their hats were decorated with large, yellow plumes. Their defiant display drew a lot of attention and eventually forced the council to rescind the order.

Four years after opening the Denver parlor house, Jennie had earned enough money to build a new brothel. In order to handle her increased business, she built an opulent, three-story, fifteen-room home. The spacious house was lavishly decorated and contained three parlors, a ballroom, dining room, large kitchen, wine cellar, and servants' quarters. The numerous clients who frequented the spectacular residence proclaimed Jennie to be the "Queen of the Row."

Law-enforcement officers visited Jennie's new place on a regular basis. She was fined several times for keeping a "noisy and disorderly house." Patrons were arrested for morphine use, and a handful of Jennie's girls were apprehended for stealing property from the men who had hired them. The constant trouble caused by the parlor houses and its residents prompted a second public outcry against the bordellos on the Row, in 1886. Politicians and townspeople again demanded that the houses be shut down. For a period of six months, officials raided the brothels, issuing fines and arresting uncooperative prostitutes. A *Denver Times* article from this period reported:

> The last few nights the police have been busily occupied among the houses of infamy, pulling [raiding] those institutions, and the result has been quite an increase in the sum paid over by the police court to the city treasury.

Jennie Rogers and fourteen other prominent madams were arrested for "keeping lewd houses." All were found guilty and were fined $75. Undeterred by the incident, Jennie and her competition were back in operation days after the raids.

Madam Rogers's insatiable appetite for the finer things drove her to some unsavory actions. With the help of one of her many lovers, she concocted a drunken, murderous scheme in order to blackmail a politician who was a parlor house regular. Jennie threatened to go public with the fact that he was a customer. The man was so convinced the information might ruin him that he agreed to pay her $17,000 to keep her quiet.

Jennie used her ill-gotten gains to build a magnificent brick and stone house. The grand brothel, which opened for business in 1889, was the talk of the West. The ceiling-to-floor mirrors that covered the walls in the reception hall earned the unique bordello the nickname "House of Mirrors," and were a topic of conversation from Denver to San Francisco. Crystal chandeliers, oriental rugs, marble tables, and grand pianos were a few of the other luxurious features.

The women Madam Rogers hired to work at her place were well groomed, had the most current hairstyles, and possessed a level of sophistication and manners not found in the average parlor house. They were also adorned in the finest fashions. Dressmakers would bring samples of their work for Jennie to see. She would then select the garments each of her employees were to wear; the cost came out of their pay. The care Jennie took to present a high-class product assured a clientele of the same refinement. Senators and legislators held meetings in the general proximity of the House of Mirrors so they could stop by Jennie's place for a visit after work.

When Jennie wasn't laboring at her trade, she was spending time with her stable of horses. She was an expert rider and could handle a coach better than most professional drivers. During one of her many weekend shopping sprees and trips to the Tabor Grand Opera House, she noticed a gruff, young hack-driver watching her every move. John A. Wood (known as Jack) was a twenty-three-year-old man who had worked around horses all his life. He was moved by Jennie's kind treatment of the animals and her ability to manage a coach. He introduced himself to her, and they became fast friends.

Jack was a poor man, lacking in pretension, and Jennie found this particular aspect of his personality irresistible. She offered to better his circumstances by purchasing a saloon for him to manage. Her sincere concern for his welfare made him fall in love with her, and in a short time, Jennie had fallen in love with him as well.

In the spring of 1887, Jennie opened a saloon in Salt Lake City, Utah. Researchers at the Denver Historical Society speculate that the location was chosen in an attempt to keep Jennie's professional life as a madam and her private life with her lover as separate as possible.

The Utah saloon was a huge success almost from the moment the doors swung open. Jennie was pleased with the way Jack handled the tavern, and she made frequent trips to oversee the operation and spend time with him. Most of her trips were planned well in advance, but on one occasion she decided to surprise her lover with an unscheduled visit. When Jennie entered Jack's living quarters, she found him with another woman. Enraged by the betrayal, Jennie pulled a pistol from a pocket in her gown and shot him. Jack's wounds were not fatal. The sheriff arrived on the scene, and Jennie was promptly arrested. When Jack was able, he told the authorities that Jennie's actions were justifiable, and she was released.

Jennie returned to Denver with a renewed commitment to bettering her already flourishing parlor houses and adding to her holdings. Using the profits made from her brothels, Madam Rogers purchased several acres of premium land in the northern portion of town. She also purchased several shares in an irrigation and reservoir project. The investment eventually yielded a tidy sum.

In spite of her increased riches and thriving businesses, Jennie was not happy. She was haunted by the image of the man she loved in the arms of another woman. The abrupt end of their relationship had not relieved Jennie of the affection she still harbored for Jack. Two years had passed since she had seen him. She thought of him often and wondered how he was doing. At the age of forty-five, she sank into a deep depression over her lost love, and visits from famous friends—like William Quayle and Marshall Field of Chicago—did nothing to improve her melancholy state.

In May of 1889, Jennie received news of Jack's whereabouts and her spirits were finally lifted. He was operating a saloon in Omaha, Nebraska. He had never married, and it was known by his many friends and acquaintances that he was still in love with Jennie. Jennie swallowed her pride and wrote Jack a letter, hoping beyond hope that he would respond. He did, and the two began a regular correspondence. By midsummer they were reunited and altar-bound. Their marriage took place on August 13, 1889.

Eight years after exchanging vows with Jennie, Jack Wood died from unknown causes. Jennie was devastated. She laid his body to rest in Denver's Fairmount Cemetery under a massive tombstone that simply read, "He is not dead, but sleeping."

Jennie tried to drown her sorrows in her work. An influx of new brothels was siphoning business away from the House of Mirrors. Madams up and down the Row had taken out ads for their establishments in a publication called the *Denver Red Book: A Reliable Directory of the Pleasure Resorts of Denver*. Some of the houses hoped to entice clients with their offers of fine wines and cigars; others listed the number of elegant rooms they had. Jennie's advertisement was a simple one. It listed a name, address, and the bold statement that "everything was first class."

Lonely and in poor health, Jennie eventually decided to lease out her parlor houses to other madams and move to the Midwest. Before departing, she was diagnosed with chronic Bright's disease, an inflammation of the filtering unit in the kidneys. She had suffered with the condition for many years, but had refused to relocate to a lower altitude, as her doctor had recommended. The ailment was now in an advanced state, and she was again strongly advised to move to a more agreeable climate.

In 1902, Jennie Rogers left the high altitude of Denver and headed to the lowlands around Chicago. Doctors ordered Jennie to stay in bed for at least seven months after she arrived, but she refused. Jennie believed the move was enough of a change for her health. She went right to work and purchased a large parlor house in the heart of Chicago. She acquired the funds for the down payment by selling off some of her Denver property and her favorite emerald earrings. In no time the new bordello was busy, and money was coming in at a rapid pace.

Her health was improving and her broken heart was on the mend. She met a charming thirty-seven-year-old contractor who captured her fancy. Archibald T. Fitzgerald was not an overly handsome man. He had dark features, a double chin, and a receding hairline, but he showered

Jennie with the attention she was craving. Their courtship was brief, but Jennie fell deeply in love with Archibald. Archibald fell deeply in love with Jennie's money.

Archibald abused the influence he had over Jennie, encouraging her to spend her fortune on expensive carriages and trips to Hot Springs, Arkansas. He convinced her that the medicinal qualities in the hot springs would bring about an instant cure for her Bright's disease. Blinded by his charisma, Jennie quickly accepted his offer of marriage after he presented her with a diamond and ruby engagement ring—a ring that was more than likely paid for with Madam Rogers's own money. Archibald and Jennie exchanged vows at Hot Springs on April 26, 1904.

Six months after the Fitzgeralds said, "I do," Jennie learned that Archibald was a bigamist. He had two other wives besides Jennie—one in Kansas City, Missouri, and the other across town in Chicago. Jennie considered divorcing Archibald several times, but he always managed to talk her out of it. The longer she stayed with him, the more money he spent. In five years, Jennie was near bankruptcy.

Consumed with worry over her finances and preoccupied with maintaining her parlor houses in Colorado and Illinois, as well as dealing with her fragile marriage, Jennie's health finally gave way. She was taken to a hospital, but nothing could be done to revive her. Jennie Rogers died on October 17, 1909. Her funeral was attended by most of the madams from the Row and several of her employees and business associates. Archibald Fitzgerald was conspicuous by his absence.

The Queen of the Colorado Red Light District was quietly buried next to her second husband. The marking on her tombstone reads, "Leah J. Wood. Died October 17, 1909." She was sixty-six years old.

ELEANORA DUMONT

GOLD COUNTRY ANGEL OF SIN

I want some excitement and a woman, I think I'll go to Madam Moustache's place.
—Miner John Bagsby, August 15, 1869

A thick fog hugged the banks of the Missouri River and clouded the docks near Fort Benton, in northern Montana. A long blast from a steamship whistle in the distance cut through the night, announcing the steamer's slow approach. The other sounds of the evening—crickets, a lonesome owl, a foraging deer—were overpowered by the competing sound of horses' hooves hurrying toward the water.

Eleven riders carrying torches raced through a thicket of trees, their silhouettes bouncing off the brush. The steamship whistle blew again. The closer it came to shore, the closer the riders advanced to the same location.

The riders charged out of the woods, arriving at a clearing that led to the wooden docks. In the open the torches illuminated the faces of the travelers. With the exception of the rider in front, all were men. Heading the group, Eleanora Dumont, a handsome woman in her late thirties, drove her horse hard. Part of her long, frizzy hair was piled high on her head, and the rest of her mane encircled her serious features. She looked like a lion on the prowl.

The incoming steamboat announced its imminent arrival with another sound of the whistle. The riders slowed their mounts to a stop and waited for the vessel to make port. The boat's captain steered the craft gently up to the dock, where three crewmembers leapt into action to weigh anchor. Before the men had a chance to step foot onto the shore, however, they were stopped by the riders, who had been awaiting their arrival. Eleanora pointed her derringer at the men, and the riders flanking her on either side leveled their guns at the sailors too.

The steamship captain stepped forward, surveying the riders and the weapons aimed at him.

"What's the meaning of this?" he shouted.

"We're here to stop you from coming any further," Eleanora firmly responded.

"And who are you?" the captain asked with a sneer.

"Madam Dumont," came the answer.

The captain thought for a moment, and then replied, "The Angel of Sin?" He motioned to her gun. "You know how to use that?"

Eleanora pulled the hammer back and fired two shots into the wood planks near the captain. "The second shot was to prove the first was no accident," she warned. "If you don't turn this boat around, the next bullet goes through your head."

"You have no right to keep the *W.B. Dance* from coming ashore," the captain proclaimed.

"We know you're carrying passengers with smallpox," Eleanora told him. "We strongly suggest you head farther down the river."

Eleanora and the other residents at Fort Benton had good reason to be cautious. In 1837, another boat carrying passengers suffering with the same sickness had docked at the exact location. More than 6,000 whites and Indians had died as a result. Madam Dumont could not allow history to be repeated.

The captain did not attempt to challenge Eleanora and her followers any further. After a few tense moments, the captain swung the wheel around and steered the steamship 130 miles down river. In four weeks' time the epidemic had run its course aboard the *W.B. Dance*. News that Eleanora had led the charge that saved thousands spread throughout the region. The notorious prostitute and brothel owner with a reputation for debauchery and lewd displays was now known for her heroism.

Legends surrounding Eleanora Dumont and her exploits began with the famed western showman and author, Ned Buntline. Like many writers he found the subject of the prostitute with a heart of gold hard to resist. Eleanora's life was filled with adventure and travel, but it paled in comparison to the tales that were later written about her.

Simone Jules, also known as Eleanora Dumont, was born in 1829. The location of her birth is not known. She claimed to be French, and her accent and mannerisms supported the assertion, but no written proof exists. What cannot be disputed is that she had a beautiful face, a flawless olive complexion, and an uncanny talent for dealing cards.

Eleanora came west with the Gold Rush, along with a small number of businesswomen who were convinced they could profit from lonely miners and their need for female companionship. She arrived in San Francisco in early 1850 and found work at the Bella Union. Among her many duties at the popular saloon, she was the house gambler. The shapely foreigner proved to be a big attraction, and soon other lady card-sharps were dealing at competing clubs. No one could compare with Eleanora, however.

In 1854, inspired by her large following, she decided to go into business for herself. She amassed a sizeable fortune during her stay in San Francisco and purchased a saloon in the booming mining community of Nevada City, California. At the age of twenty-five, she opened the doors of her own place and welcomed a flood of thirsty argonauts. Dumont's gambling den on Main Street was unique in many ways. In addition to the fact that the proprietor was a well-known lady gambler from the Barbary Coast, food and champagne were offered free to the customers and were served around the clock.

Eleanora's specialty was dealing Twenty-One, or Blackjack. In her flinty, singsong voice, she would invite card players to "have a go" at *vingt-et-un,* the French translation of the game. Patrons were so busy talking with the charming Madam Dumont during the round that they scarcely noticed when they'd lost. Losers who were good sports were treated like royalty by the women who worked in Eleanora's upstairs brothel. Keeping customers happy and in good humor despite losing their money ensured repeat business.

When Eleanora wasn't dealing, she mingled with the rowdy clientele, flirting and flattering, rolling cigarettes and pouring drinks. Outside of her business Madam Dumont conducted herself with the utmost propriety. She was always appropriately dressed, polite, and careful to never appear snobbish or withdrawn. She graciously declined the advances of amorous miners who hoped to "make an honest woman" out of her. Her evenings were spent alone in her room at the National Hotel.

Nevada County historians note that the sophisticated Eleanora harbored a deep love for Editor Waite of the *Nevada Journal*. She adored him and longed for the respectability that he offered. Waite, however, did not return Eleanora's affections. There were occasional late-night calls to her hotel room, but outside of fulfilling a basic need, Waite had no further use for her. The ultimate demise of their relationship came after Waite married a "socially acceptable" woman. Eleanora would never get over the loss.

With her heart broken and business falling off (due to rumors of gold being played out in the region), Eleanora was left both emotionally and professionally vulnerable. Enter Lucky David Tobin. Tobin, a tall man with devilish good looks, was an itinerate gambler. Not long after introducing himself to the French beauty, he persuaded her to take him on as a partner in her struggling establishment. Tobin immediately began making improvements. He added keno tables, roulette wheels, and a faro bank. Dumont's place flourished once again.

Rumors circulated among the patrons of Eleanora's gambling hall that she and Lucky Dave were more than business associates. But Eleanora continued to harbor deep feelings for Editor Waite, and Dave was involved with more than one woman in Nevada City.

As business continued to improve, Lucky Dave became more and more greedy, demanding a higher cut of the profits. At first Eleanora tried to accommodate her partner, but as time went on she decided against giving in to his demands. In a heated discussion one evening, Eleanora informed Lucky Dave that she didn't need a man. She had gotten along fine prior to his assistance and would do so again. The partners went their separate ways. Tobin took his huge share of earned profits and headed to New York.

Madam Dumont did not linger long after Lucky Dave left. In 1856, news of the rich Comstock Lode in Nevada reached the mining community, and Eleanora decided to go where more money could be made. She sold the business, deciding to follow the various gold and silver strikes throughout the West. Her vagabond lifestyle would span two decades.

For the first year she traveled from one boomtown to another. Eleanora's presence in mining camps like Columbia threatened gamblers who had established successful businesses. In spite of the criticism and the strong suggestion that she leave, Eleanora played the gambling tables, winning big the majority of the time.

From Columbia, California, she moved to Idaho, stopping off long enough in gold-mining towns like Orofino, Florence, and Boise City to win large sums of money. She used her winnings to purchase other gambling houses. Eleanora was well received everywhere she shuffled a deck of cards. Men liked her, and her presence made the long evenings away from their families back east bearable.

By 1864, she was sharing her talents with argonauts in Bannack, Montana. She purchased a fancy, two story place that had a saloon downstairs and a brothel upstairs. Among the many young women who worked to keep the miners' winnings in the house was a fifteen-year-old girl named Martha Jane Cannary. Martha Jane, better known as Calamity Jane, was one of the Wild West's most notorious characters.

Madam Dumont's time in any one place was brief. After her stay in Bannack, she moved on to Bozeman, then to Fort Benton. In 1867, she added railroad construction camps to her itinerary of stopovers. She followed the Union Pacific workers throughout Wyoming and back to Nevada.

Historical records indicate that somewhere on her journey, between 1865 and 1868, she met, married, and divorced a cattle buyer named Jack McKnight. The pair settled on a ranch near Carson City, Nevada, and for a while they were happy. The blissful union ended when McKnight abruptly left, taking all of Eleanora's money with him. Alone and destitute, she was forced back into a life of gambling and prostitution.

Madam Dumont began drinking heavily to deal with her heartache. Lines of grief and desperation marred her beautiful face. Her features coarsened, and a growth of dark hair appeared on her upper lip. Unsympathetic men she encountered in towns and camps ridiculed her looks and conferred upon her the title of "Madam Moustache." Although she tried to hide it, the handle cut deep.

In 1867, Madam Dumont returned to San Francisco, where her career had begun, and opened another parlor house. Her excessive drinking had affected her skill at cards, but patrons continued to seek her out and challenge her to games. She still managed to win the majority of hands, and most maintained that they "would rather lose to Madam Dumont than win from any male tin-horn."

Not everyone appreciated Eleanora's notoriety. Some men resented being taken by a woman at cards and looked forward to the day when her career would end and she would leave town altogether. In the fall of 1869, she did leave San Francisco, and stage magician John Henry Anderson remarked:

> Mlle. Dumont has apparently gone out of business. I was told that early this morning carriages took the ladies and their baggage, and shortly after dinner the proprietress was seen departing, without a word to anyone, as perhaps fitting. A man came later this afternoon and took those two loads of chairs, but not the beds.

After departing San Francisco, Eleanora headed back to Montana, where she frequented such locations as Virginia City and Last Chance

Gulch. From there Madam Dumont took her business back to Idaho and towns like Murray, Coeur d'Alene, and Eagle City, then on to Deadwood, South Dakota, and Cheyenne, Wyoming. At each stop Eleanora kept an eye out for her ex-husband, Jack McKnight. Her pistol was always close at hand in case she saw him. She promised herself that if their paths ever crossed, she'd put a bullet in the man who had stolen her heart and her money.

At the age of fifty, her card-playing talents and beauty fading, Eleanora decided to move her game to Bodie, California. A gold strike there had made the tough northern California camp a popular destination for ambitious miners.

Madam Dumont arrived in the bustling town in September of 1879. After enjoying more than a few drinks at one of the thirty saloons in the small town, Eleanora staggered over to a twenty-one table and began playing. By the end of the evening, she had lost all of her money.

Sitting in the back of the Grand Central Saloon, Eleanora contemplated how far she'd come from the profitable days she had once enjoyed in Nevada City. She thought about all she had lost, and her mind settled on Editor Waite. She sunk into a deep depression. The bartender offered her a bottle of whiskey and she didn't refuse. Maybe she could drink her memories away.

On the morning of September 8, Madam Dumont's dead body was found outside of town. An empty vial of poison was discovered nearby, and clutched in her hand was a tear-stained note, requesting that she be buried next to Editor Waite. Newspapers across the West posted the famous gambler's obituary, graciously omitting from their report the cruel nickname of Madam Moustache. The *Sacramento Union* reported:

> A woman named Eleanora Dumont was found dead today about one mile out of town, having committed suicide. She was well known through all the mining camps. Let her many good qualities invoke leniency in criticizing her failings.

Bodie townspeople and saloon owners took up a collection for Eleanora's burial. They were able to raise enough money to bury her in Bodie, and would not allow her to be laid to rest in the "outcast cemetery."

MADAM HARRIET

A CURIOUS CRIMINAL CASE

Prostitutes, by nature of their profession, often found themselves in trouble with the law. It was not uncommon for a lady of the evening to be accused of blackmail, theft, or even murder. Such was the case of a soiled dove in Northern California accused of murdering a miner. The curious criminal proceedings were held before Justice John Anderson in 1852, and an article in an August edition of the *Union Times* attempted to unravel the mystery for its readers:

A public woman, popularly known as "Old Harriet," kept a saloon on Broad Street, overlooking Deer Creek. She had a man, who kept bar for her, and did any necessary fighting. Opposite her establishment was a dance house. A man named Pat Berry was mining on the opposite side of Deer Creek at Gold Run. Owing to a recent freshet, there were no bridges at the foot of the town, but a tree had been cleared of limbs and felled across it, over which foot passengers made their way. The stream was still high, and raged among the naked boulders and logs, which were then innocent of tailings.

On Saturday Berry came over to town, having made some money during the week, and rigged himself out with an entire new outfit of clothing. He spent the evening until late at the dance house and then went over to Old Harriet's place, which was the last ever seen of him alive.

In the course of the night, a man in the neighborhood heard what he took to be a cry of "murder," but he may have been mistaken. Two or three days after, about six miles below Nevada, in an eddy in the creek, Berry's body was found, completely naked. On the forehead was a large, extravagated wound, the blood discoloration proving that this wound was given while the person was alive. Finding him in this condition led to search for previous traces of him; and it was discovered that he had passed the evening at the dance house, and then gone to Old Harriet's, where all further trace of him was lost.

Harriet and her fighting man were arrested and charged before the Justice with murder. McConnell prosecuted and Sawyer defended. The examination lasted several days. The prosecution proved that Berry had money, traced his movements the night of his death, as herein stated, showed that the wound on his head must have been given while he was alive, and that it was made with some round, blunt weapon; that there was a pair of scales on Old Harriet's counter, and a large weight, which would produce such a wound; the condition of the body, with a new, strong suit of clothes entirely missing; which, it was contended it was impossible could be torn off by the stream, or at least, without greatly marring the body, which was intact, except the death wound on the head. The cry of murder was also proven, leaving a close knitted theory by the prosecution, well sustained before the drowning. As to the missing clothes, it was argued, though with less confidence, that they had been stripped off by the water, rocks, and logs.

The case was so puzzling that the Justice took it under advisement for several days. While he was considering it, two men walked the log in company, when one of them pitched off and disappeared. Everybody turned out to find the body, but the search was unsuccessful for several days, when it was found in the eddy below the town from which Berry's body was taken. The head of the new victim was marked with the same kind of extravagated wound as that of the first one, but there were no other wounds on the body, and all his clothes were gone except his shirt, which was turned inside out and hung at the wrist. The case was at once reopened and this evidence of what might happen was submitted. When she heard the new testimony Old Harriet exclaimed: "The Lord has intervened to save an innocent woman!" Of course the accused went free.

JESSIE HAYMAN

THE SAN FRANCISCO FAVORITE

*She had the face and figure of an empress, and the poise
and manner of one as well.*
—Description of Jessie Hayman
by the Grand Duke of Russia, 1908

Jessie Hayman turned down the flame of the gas lamp that sat atop a
giant fireplace mantle in the parlor of her well-known brothel. Apart
from the light filtering in from the red lantern hanging off the porch, the
room was blanketed in darkness. It was almost 4 A.M., and all of the
home's boarders were settled in their rooms with their overnight guests.

Madam Hayman's palatial bordello was one of the most popular
businesses in San Francisco in 1906. Thirty attractive women of various
ages and nationalities worked for Jessie. The income earned from her
employees totaled more than $4,000 a night. Consequently, Jessie was
one of the wealthiest madams in the city.

As Jessie went about the routine of closing up shop, a heavy knock
on the front door startled her. It was late for callers, but not outside the
realm of possibility. As she made her way to the foyer, she removed a pistol from a pocket on her dress. She cocked the gun just as she opened
the door, and raised it even with the face of a portly man standing opposite her. The stunned man threw his hands up and took a step back.

"If you're a gentleman caller who got a late start, please forgive
me," Jessie stated firmly. "But if you've come to rob the place, you've
got to get past me first."

After apologizing for the intrusion and assuring Jessie that he was merely interested in the company of one of her ladies, the frazzled man was allowed inside. Before Jessie had an opportunity to ask about his preferences, he hurried off up the stairs. He seemed to know exactly where he was going.

"Guess he's been here before," she said to herself. "Wouldn't do to shoot a regular."

Once she made sure all the doors and windows were locked, she retired to her enormous bedroom. Eight hours later she would open the house again and greet patrons with an enthusiastic smile, hearty handshake, and a pistol in her pocket. "I keep my customers close and my gun closer," she told friends and family. "It's helped me settle many an argument."

Jessie Hayman was born in 1867, in New Orleans, Louisiana. Her parents, Thad and Constance Wyant, named her Annie May. Very little is known of her childhood.

Historians at the California Historical Library speculate that her family headed west when Annie was a young girl. They died of cholera while en route to the Gold Country, and the orphan eventually turned to prostitution in desperation. For years she traveled about the various mining camps and cow towns, working as a public woman. Census records indicate that Annie arrived in San Francisco in 1891. By then she was known as Jessie Mellon.

Jessie was the most sought-after boarder of the resorts on Ellis and Post Streets. Nina Hayman was the madam of those houses and she became Jessie's mentor. Nina was kind and patient with her and treated her like a daughter. Jessie was a tall, slender woman with red hair and a bottom that men said was "something to watch." She also had a good head for business. Nina encouraged her protégé's talents and promised to help Jessie establish her own house. In 1898, Nina left the trade and married a wealthy lumber dealer. As a parting gift she made good on her promise and turned the brothel over to Jessie. Out of gratitude for her mentor's actions, the thirty-one-year-old Jessie took her madam's last name as her own.

The new Madam Hayman retained the sophisticated air of the three-story home, but enhanced the champagne concession in the ballroom. A larger variety of imported, high-priced wines were offered and were served in fine, diamond-cut crystal. The much-talked-about stemware earned her the nickname "Diamond Jessie."

Jessie's gilded palace was frequented by commoners and royalty alike. A few princes, czars, and dukes from visiting countries paid visits to the resort. In 1899, the Grand Duke of the Imperial Russian Empire spent time with the lovely Madam Hayman and a few of her employees. He was reportedly so enthralled by Jessie's beauty that he invited her to return with him to his homeland. Jessie declined the gracious offer. He then commissioned a life-sized painting of her before he "left American soil."

The twelve to twenty women in Jessie's employ thought highly of her. Most of them paid $5 a day for room and board. Clients were charged $5 to be entertained. Women who were popular, young (fourteen and under), and in possession of certain "special" abilities, charged more for their services and consequently paid more for food and shelter. The average workday hours were from noon to four in the morning. Before the girls retired, they bathed in lavender salts and were treated to a massage by the housemaids.

The chorus of girls in Jessie's care considered her to be the best madam in the business. She was kind and fair, but strict and honest in all her business dealings. One of the house favorites boasted that "Jessie was the tops, and when you worked for her, you were tops in the business."

Jessie's reputation for being a good madam attracted many girls to her parlor house. She always had more applicants than available positions. Many wanted to work for her because they had heard how generous she was to her staff. If more than average amounts of alcohol were consumed during special parties and celebrations, Jessie paid her girls a 5 percent commission from the profits. The girls were also allowed to keep any tips they made for serving clients meals cooked at the house.

Jessie gave a lot to her boarders, but she also expected much in return. Her girls were required to act ladylike at all times, to keep themselves clean and neat, and to wear clothing that reflected the high quality of the house. A boarder's wardrobe had to first be approved by Jessie. If her clothing did not fit the ideal the madam had in mind, she had to buy new garments. Jessie advanced her girls the money necessary to purchase the gowns they needed. The wardrobe consisted of a number of expensive items, including:

1 fox fur for suits	$300.00
4 tailored suits	$100.00 each
4 street dresses	$75.00 each
8 hats for street	$15.00 each
2 dress coats	$250.00 each
12 pair street shoes	$18.00 each
4½ dozen hose	$5.00 pair
6 pocketbooks	$10.00 each
2 evening bags	$10.00 each
½ dozen gloves, day	$8.00 pair
½ dozen gloves, evening	$12.50 pair
7 evening gowns	$100.00 each
7 negligees	$75.00 each
12 teddy slips	$18.00 each
24 night gowns	$20.00 each
6 pair mules	$15.00 each
2 evening wraps	$750.00 each
7 pair evening shoes	$15.00 each
9 dozen handkerchiefs	$11.50 dozen
6 blouses	$10.00 each
TOTAL	$6,088.50

In addition to paying for the clothing, deductions were taken from the women's earnings to pay the mistress for maintaining the business and to pay for three full-time maids. A portion of a prostitute's salary also went to pay for doctor examinations, weekly laundry services, and police payoffs. Jessie was a meticulous bookkeeper and provided her ladies with a weekly account of their finances.

Madam Hayman's attention to detail helped make her resorts the San Francisco favorite. Customers enjoyed the company of the lovely staff and the services they provided. When they arose they found their clothes cleaned and pressed, their shoes shined, and an appetizing breakfast awaiting them. Jessie used the money she made from the house and the extras she provided to purchase numerous parcels of land throughout the city.

On April 18, 1906, Jessie and her boarders were shaken out of their beds at five in the morning by a violent earthquake. Her home on Post Street was ruined, but apart from the chimney that had toppled over, the parlor house on Ellis Street suffered little damage. The same could not be said for the majority of the city, however. San Francisco was in ruins, not only from the quakes but also from the subsequent fires. Twenty-eight thousand structures were destroyed over 490 blocks. A quarter of a million people were left homeless, and 450 were dead.

Madam Hayman, and many other brothel owners and their employees, took it upon themselves to help care for the injured and dying. They helped feed and clothe thousands of homeless who had gathered at the Golden Gate Park and had no place else to go.

Very few parlor houses were left standing after the Great Earthquake of 1906. Jessie quickly recognized the inherent business opportunity, and rebuilt her Post Street house, adding a new wing to her bordello and hiring ten more girls. Neighbors in the area complained to city officials about the late-night activity at Madam Hayman's. Once the city had begun the process of rebuilding, the level of tolerance for such an establishment had decreased. Politicians were pressured to crack down on those police who accepted payoffs to overlook prostitution. District Attorney William L. Langdon agreed, and in the fall of 1906, he waged war against the brothel patrons and owners. Langdon was specifically interested in apprehending the wealthiest madam in the business. He issued a warrant for Jessie and put the profession on notice that her arrest was only the beginning.

Jessie was humiliated by the arrest and insulted by the press's claim that she was a "notorious woman in the underworld." After paying the $200 bail, she left the jail and went back to work. She vowed that it would take more than an arrest to force her out of business.

The following year, a scandal involving a saloon owner and a prominent San Francisco landowner prompted Jessie to close the doors of her Post Street house. When news spread that the respectable landowner had been frequently seen at Jessie's brothel and was helping to fund an addition to the house, the pair became the talk of the town. Not only did Jessie's partner deny their association, but he also joined forces with the proprietor of the saloon next door and persuaded politicians to shut down Jessie's house. After the demise of the parlor house on Post Street, Jessie devoted all of her time and attention to her Ellis Street business.

Federal laws at the time prohibited the hiring of immigrants who had been in the United States less than three years. Many of Jessie's boarders were from France and Russia, and this statute prevented her from running her day-to-day operations as she normally did. Immigration officials felt the code needed to extend to parlor house operators. Jessie Hayman was the first madam to be arrested for hiring illegal immigrants.

On August 25, 1908, United States marshals raided Jessie's newest home on Mason Street and found an Englishwoman who had only been in the country for three months working there. Both she and Jessie were arrested. Jessie's $10,000 bond was posted by several prominent men who had spent a great deal of time at her parlor houses.

While awaiting trial on charges of "harboring and maintaining an alien in a house of ill fame," Jessie witnessed the arrest of several other madams in the city. Local police could still be bought off, but federal officials no longer allowed themselves to be manipulated. Within six months the majority of bordello owners and operators, who had spent a fortune on bribing police and government officials, were arrested and carted off to jail.

At the trial, Jessie took the stand in her own defense and testified that the young woman working for her was not a prostitute, but an entertainer who had been hired to sing and perform on the piano. The federal officers testified differently and submitted proof that the young girl was indeed a prostitute who had worked for several parlor houses throughout the West before settling at Jessie's place. Jessie cried and pleaded with the jury to believe her, but they were not persuaded. Jessie was found guilty and sentenced to a $300 fine and 30 days in jail.

Madam Hayman served her time at a prison in Alameda, then returned to work at yet another house on Mason Street.

After remaining there for a short time, she decided to close the location and open a new business across town. Jessie's grand establishment on Eddy Street was another three-story building with three fireplaces, a saloon, fifteen suites, a dining room, and a massive kitchen. According to Beverly Davis, a boarder who lived and worked at the location, the interior was an impressive site:

> She had a champagne cellar with wine from all parts of the world. Whoever furnished the house knew his stuff. There was a red room, the Turkish room, the French room, the blue room. Oriental couches and shaded lamps, such plush rooms, one after another with deep carpets on the floor. The bedroom upstairs was done in the best style. It reflected the tone of the parlor house all the way through.

The number of boarders at Madam Hayman's Eddy Street location varied between twelve to fifteen women. In 1912, all of the ladies in her employ were Americans. The list of residents included two girls from Tennessee, one from Kentucky, three from Missouri, two from Colorado, one from Nebraska, four from California, and two sisters, who were Comanche Indians from Texas.

After sixteen years as a San Francisco madam, Jessie Hayman retired and decided to travel the world. She toured a variety of countries including Japan, China, India, Palestine, and Egypt. On March 31, 1923, in a hotel room in London, she died from a massive heart attack. A maid found Jessie seated in a chair. She was elegantly dressed for dinner and wearing many of the diamonds she had acquired over her lifetime. The fifty-six-year-old ex-madam never married. She left the bulk of her $116,000 estate to her eight-year-old niece, her five brothers and sisters, and her two cats.

JESSIE REEVES AND CAD THOMPSON

SCARLET LADIES IN TEXAS AND NEVADA

Teacher, this woman was caught in the act of adultery.
In the Law Moses commanded us to stone such women.
Now what do you say?

—*John 8:4-5*

On July 12, 1900, several well-dressed guests filtered into a giant Salvation Army tent in New York City and found seats among the rows of wooden crates. A steady breeze rustled the sides of the canvas enclosure, but offered no relief from the oppressive summer heat. Few allowed themselves to be distracted by the uncomfortable conditions. They had come to hear a message from the former prostitute Jessie Reeves, and nothing could drive them from the setting. Once the audience was settled, the speaker approached the lectern.

Jessie Reeves was an attractive, but hard-looking, woman. The creases around her dark features made her look every bit her forty-plus years. Her eyes, though tired, reflected an inner peace. The congregation watched her every move closely. Jessie placed a well-worn Bible on the lectern and stared out at the eager crowd.

For more than an hour, she shared the details of her sordid past, describing her days as a prostitute-turned-madam in an area known as Hell's Half Acre in Fort Worth, Texas. She described her sinful deeds and the shady characters she had known with rich detail. After painting a bleak picture of a vile past, she shared how her life had been transformed.

"I was out for my mid-day constitutional when I happened by the open doorway of a small house," she explained. "I heard someone inside singing hymns and I was drawn to the sweet message in the music." Jessie entered the home and met the gospel minister who lived there. He told her about God and how he forgave sins. "I took the Savior into my soul that day," she happily proclaimed. "And I turned over a new leaf."

The audience was riveted by her tale of change. Hurting, troubled men and women rushed the pulpit at the conclusion of the service. Her words had turned their hearts.

Given the fact that historians have been unable to determine her real name, little has been uncovered about the early life of Jessie Reeves. According to a handful of historical records, Jessie was born and raised in Spain. She arrived in Fort Worth in 1881 with her sister. Once in the United States, Jessie took on a variety of jobs, which included working as a circus performer and a faro dealer. Her faro-dealing days were marred with violence and injury. After losing all of his money gambling one evening, an angry cowboy shot Jessie in the chest. He accused her of dealing off the bottom of the deck. It took fifteen months for the wound to completely heal, but Jessie did survive the ordeal.

By 1885, Jessie was operating her own parlor house, located across the street from the home of another famous Texas madam, Mary Porter. It was here that Jessie and her staff tended to the needs of many respectable and prominent citizens. Among the notable members of society who frequented her business was a well-known rancher and oil-man who was romantically linked to Madam Reeves for many years.

Jessie was arrested several times over the course of her career. The charges ranged from operating a disorderly house to vagrancy. She was required to pay more than $600 a year in fines.

Madam Reeves's reputation was not solely tied to her profession. She was also known for her generosity toward the homeless, destitute children, police officers, and firemen. In the summer of 1888, a boarding house across from her business caught fire and threatened to destroy the entire town. Jessie sent supplies of food and blankets to the firefighters to help sustain them in their efforts. Many buildings surrounding her house burned to the ground, but Jessie's home was spared.

In 1867, Virginia City, Nevada, madam Cad Thompson found herself in similar circumstances, but she wasn't as fortunate as Jessie Reeves. Of course Cad did not possess the benevolent spirit Jessie had either.

Caroline (Cad) Thompson was born Sarah Hagen in Ireland in 1827. Not long after her husband passed away, Cad moved to Virginia City with her five-year-old son Henry. As a result of the discovery of silver and gold in the area, the northern Nevada mining town was booming. Cad was a shrewd businesswoman who determined early on that she could capitalize on the lustful miners' need for women. She purchased a large, two-story brick house, moved five attractive ladies in, and invited the public to one of the town's most elegant parlor houses.

Madam Thompson's house was commonly referred to as "The Brick." It was elegantly furnished with items from San Francisco and Paris. Among the many features of the home were separate rooms for each boarder and a piano parlor.

Cad's business was always open. She hosted a steady stream of men twenty-four hours a day. The loud, drunken noises and music emanating from the home at all hours of the night prompted neighbors to level complaints to law enforcement officers. Cad was subsequently arrested many times for disturbing the peace, and for drunk and disorderly conduct. To protest what she felt was harassment, she often refused to pay the fines associated with the conviction, opting instead to be jailed.

Cad's personal life was just as troubled as her professional one. In 1864, she became romantically involved with an Irish stonemason named John Dalton. John had been arrested for fighting as often as Cad had been arrested for drunk and disorderly conduct. The violent tempers and stubbornness they both possessed made for a lethal combination. Cad had John arrested for assault a number of times, but would eventually bail him out. The two would then reconcile and start the process over again.

On July 4, 1867, a fight between John and Cad resulted in gunplay. John threatened Cad's life, and she pulled a derringer out to defend herself. He wrestled the gun from her just as the police arrived at the scene. An officer entered the home and shot and killed John. Cad claimed the officer had murdered her lover, but he was found to have acted in self-defense.

Madam Thompson not only fought with her customers and romantic interests, but with other prostitutes as well. Mary Livingston, a popular boarder, worked for Cad. When the two got into a disagreement over a minor issue, the argument escalated into a shouting match. Cad demanded that Mary vacate the premises. Mary refused, and a fistfight occured. Cad beat the young woman to a pulp and threw her out. Mary pressed charges and a trial ensued.

Members of the male jury listened to the testimony and decided to acquit Cad. The men in the gallery who were moved by Mary's sad tale of abuse at the hand of Cad were furious with the madam. They pledged to get even with Cad for hurting Mary. The men devised a plan to set fire to Madam Thompson's place and force her out of business, then sounded the alarm. Firemen responded to the growing inferno and flooded the property with water. The interior of the house was ruined. A neighbor, Alf Doten, noted in his journal that Cad had been the victim of a "well-calculated vendetta." He went on to describe the scene:

> Some fellows took No. 1's engine about 4 o'clock this morning and washed out old Cad Thompson's whore house—gave her hell—created quite a consternation among the law and order portion of the community—not the end of it yet. We shall have to see who rules the city not the rough or the decent men.

Cad rebuilt "The Brick" and purchased two other houses. Eleven years after the fire, her only child committed suicide. Henry was a twenty-two-year-old alcoholic. In August of 1878, he shot himself in the chest. He was still clinging to life when the doctor arrived to tend to his wound. Henry shunned any attempts at saving him and told the doctor, "If I had wanted to live, it is not very likely that I would have shot myself."

Cad retired from the business in 1892. History records note that Madam Thompson and "The Brick" were among the most popular attractions in Virginia City.

This 1905 illustration aptly depicts one of the harsh realities of a life of prostitution. Entitled, "Where's Mabel?" it shows a parlor-house patron enquiring of the madam about the whereabouts of one of the popular girls in her employ. The brutal answer was, "She has croaked." The upper part of the picture shows the burial of the girl in a potter's field.

This 1908 photograph of a back alleyway in San Francisco's Red Light District reveals the harsh conditions some "crib girls" lived with.

Nellie was one of more than 600 prostitutes in San Francisco in the mid-1870s. She worked at Tessie Wall's parlor house.

LICENSE FOR PROSTITUTION.

No. 14

TO ALL WHO SHALL SEE THESE PRESENTS—GREETING:

Know Ye, That whereas, *Buffalo Sue*

on the 10 day of *May* 1876, paid to the City Secretary the sum of Two Dollars and Fifty Cents ($2.50), being the license imposed on a PROSTITUTE, and otherwise complied with the regulations of the City Ordinances in this behalf.

Therefore, the said *Buffalo Sue* is hereby authorized and empowered to follow said occupation or business for the term of THREE MONTHS, from the 10 day of *May* 1876

In Testimony Whereof, I have hereunto set my hand and caused the Seal of the City to be affixed, at the Secretary's office, in said City, this 10 day of *May* 1876

Expires 10 day of *August*

NOT TRANSFERABLE.

In some areas, prostitutes were required to buy and post licenses.

Posting a photograph alongside a prostitute's license was an advertising ploy.

Texas Tommy, AKA Rose Ellis, poses with her dog in 1923.

Enticing photographs were often hung in the parlors of the brothels to tempt clients.

Eleanora Dumont, AKA Madam Mustache, was unafraid to use her pistol to defend herself.

Though appearing demure in this studio portrait, Jennie Rogers declared herself, "Queen of the Colorado Underworld."

Mattie Silks, Queen of Denver's Red Light District, in the finery her business sense allowed her to afford.

Kate Horony, known as Big Nose Kate, was infamous throughout the West as a madam—but also for her relationship with the equally infamous Doc Holliday.

JOSIE WASHBURN

NEBRASKA'S RELUCTANT MADAM

*From reckless despair she drifted into the life; it is with
determination bordering on reckless that she starts to
quit it.*

—Josie Washburn,
on the reformation of a prostitute, 1905

A large wagon filled with prostitutes rattled down a rocky street in
Lincoln, Nebraska. It was daylight, but a hard rain obscured the sun.
Three armed sheriff's deputies walked alongside the crowded vehicle,
grinning from ear to ear. Raindrops bounced off the tin badges pinned
to their slickers. The drenched passengers huddled together like chick-
ens caught in a storm.

Dignified citizens stared out of shop windows and saloon doors at
the public women under arrest, who were being paraded through town.
Some of the humiliated prostitutes hid their faces with scarves; others
hung their heads in shame. Josie Washburn, a pretty, neatly dressed
brunette in the center of the wagon, kept her eyes fixed on the gawking
residents. Her pride was wounded, but she refused to give them the satisfaction of letting them see she'd been broken.

The ride to the jail was slow and deliberate. Lightning streaked
across the sky, and the rain fell in sheets. As the wagon passed by the
bank, two businessmen stepped into the doorframe and laughed at the
sight of the soaked women. Their insensitive chortles fanned the flames
of Josie's rage, and at once she was on her feet. "You don't think we have

feelings?!" she shouted. "We may be whores, but we have feelings just like anyone else."

Thunder rolled overhead. Josie glanced around at the stunned onlookers. "You need us to protect the good women here, you say!" she bellowed over the sound of the violent weather. "And you treat us like livestock!"

One of the deputies ordered her to "sit down and shut up." Josie glared at him. He leveled his shotgun at her and pumped the barrel. "Go ahead," she dared him. "Put me out of their misery."

Until Josie Washburn was motivated to do so, virtually no one spoke out on behalf of public women. They were talked about, mistreated, and shunned by society, but little understanding was given to why some women were driven to prostitution. Josie's lone voice and extensive writing on the subject exposed the conditions that perpetuated the profession.

Josie Washburn began working at parlor houses in Omaha, Nebraska, in August of 1871. She was seventeen years old. Born in the Northeast to parents of Scottish and Norwegian descent, she was given the name Helena. However, Anna Wilson, the first madam the young girl worked for, changed Helena's name to one that was more suitable for the trade. Historians speculate that Josie was abandoned at an early age and forced to make her own way. Job opportunities for women were limited at the time, and desperation and the threat of starvation led many to the profession.

Anna's brothel was a home for Josie and the other girls who worked there. For many of them it was the first time they felt they belonged somewhere. In spite of the dire circumstances, a sense of family prevailed among the residents of the house. Josie stayed at Anna's for more than eight years.

Josie was arrested numerous times on prostitution charges during her time of employment at Madam Wilson's. The public humiliation of being dragged into court time after time eventually took its toll on her. The shame she felt for the life she was forced to live overshadowed the devotion she had for Anna and the other women at the house. Unable to continue on, Josie attempted to kill herself using a borrowed revolver. Her unsteady hand caused the weapon to miss its intended mark, and as a result she suffered a non-fatal bullet wound. Newspaper reports claimed the shooting was an accident.

A proposal of marriage gave Josie the chance to escape her sad lifestyle. When she exchanged vows with Frank Stone in early 1880, she believed her future had great promise. Stone was an educated man, and Josie was deeply in love with him. Frank proved to be anything but reliable, however. For fifteen years the pair drifted from one western town to the next. He was bad with money and gambled large sums away. He frequently left his wife alone for months at a time. Josie was devastated by his actions and later wrote about her disappointment:

A man expects his wife to be an angel under any and all circumstances. The man pledges his protection, care, and love for life, and upon these terms the woman becomes his wife, in full confidence that this love is permanent and lasting; in sickness or health she has a right to expect him to be true to her.

The great burden of married life comes to the wife, who has her household duties, and the children to care for, and a thousand and one things to perform which make up the daily routine.

When the husband comes home from his daily occupation, his wife has a right to expect his company during the evening; to her his presence is company, even though he chooses to bury himself in his newspapers.

But she does not receive this consideration. He is absent night after night and often until the break of day, or for several days. When he arrives he is nervous and grouchy, and throws things around. While he is changing his wearing apparel he loses the proverbial collar buttons, strewing them upon the floor, and cussing because they are not as large as sledgehammers. A man in that condition isn't noted for his nimble fingers among other deficiencies. His wife comes to his rescue, fastens his collar, and observes that his breath hasn't the aroma of violets, nor his blood-shot eyes the expression of remorse; he does not make the effort to hold his temper that he did the collar-button. With a scowl he tells his wife that he has been at a banquet.

He remains at home for a night or two to rest up. Then he goes to another banquet, or club, or he is called away from town on a matter of business, or important transactions kept him at the office, or he met some friends at a hotel who detained him; he volunteers this information without any interrogations from his wife, who trembles with fear that something is wrong. When men go out in bunches, they sometimes frankly admit to their wives that they have been out with the boys seeing the sights, but they don't tell what they saw.

In 1895, Frank Stone abandoned Josie for good. He left her with numerous debts and no viable income. She was forced to return to the type of work she often referred to as the "underworld sewer." Josie settled in Lincoln, Nebraska, and after earning a substantial amount of money working as a prostitute, she opened her own parlor house. Historical records show that she had five employees in June of 1900. The clients who frequented her business were from all walks of life— politicians and pioneers, preachers and police.

Josie took her job as madam seriously, looking out for the ladies in her hire in much the same way Anna Wilson had looked after her. According to Josie's memoirs, "a wise matron of the underworld is a woman of many resources and sound judgment, which is gained by experience so severe that you would not believe it possible for a human being to endure." Josie treated her staff with kindness and respect, and protected them from violent men, drug sellers, thieves, and gamblers. "The madam is the best friend a girl has," Josie wrote in her autobiography. "And it is generally so admitted by the girl who believes in being anywhere near decent."

Josie did her best to look out for her boarders' well-being, but she could not protect them from the "violations" she was sure they would encounter once the bedroom door had closed behind them. She believed that prostitutes "lost a bit of their soul each time they entertained a client." Those new to the profession harbored the misconception that the wealthier a client was, the better he would treat the women. In her writings, Josie made it clear that the opposite was true:

> Upon the first arrival of the girl, she imagines that all her troubles will be gone when she becomes acquainted with the rich man, but there is no class of men who are less generous than the rich man when he is sober, although he will spend thousands of dollars for self-indulgence, buying champagne by the case. He will order all that the bunch can drink, waste, lave, and wallow in.
>
> The girls are required to take a part in the lowest debauchery, for the amusement of this man, for which they are liberally supplied with money, besides the madam's rake-off isn't small; through all kinds of confusion she never loses sight of the business at hand.
>
> After a girl has been through one of these orgies with the rich man, there is nothing left in the line of vice that is not familiar to her. A girl might be in some parts of the underworld for years, and not have the knowledge or experience in vice that these girls have learned under the direction of one rich man, in a week or a month's extreme revelry.

Prostitution in Nebraska in the early 1900s was lucrative work, and Josie Washburn's house made a great deal of money. She and her girls were required to pay large sums to public officials to stay in operation, however. As the madam, Josie was required to pay a monthly protection fee to local law enforcement of $14.70 to $29.70. Officers varied in the ways they collected the payments. Some were satisfied with allowing Josie to submit the payment through a messenger. Others required individual prostitutes to pay the fee in person at the jail.

Women who did not have the money owed were thrown into a cell and held there until their bill was paid. "We always went [to the jail] with fear and trembling," Josie wrote:

> Whenever law enforcement wanted to prove to the public at large that prostitution was not being tolerated, they would load women from various parlor houses into a mud wagon and parade them through town. We regarded this treatment as unjust and cruel, but the effect was to make us more willing to part with our cash.

Opportunities for employment for men were vast. They could take any career path they wanted. Frontier women did not have the same advantages. So when men chose to own and operate a brothel, Josie was highly resentful. She considered "he-landladies" or "P.I.s" (an abbreviation for pimp) to be the most despicable member of the underworld:

> There is one [P.I.] in the city of Omaha who owns the greater share of the red-light district, which is of no small proportions in this city.
>
> This he-landlady leases and controls several alleys, on which he has built rows of cribs, both sides similarly arranged. Each crib consists of two small rooms, about six feet high; a door and a window forms the whole front. Each crib has a projecting corner, and a casual glance down the line gives it a scalloped appearance, which is meant to be artistic. . . .
>
> Some of the girls who exist in these alleys are those who have seen years of suffering, and are now addicted to dope and liquor. But the majority are the very young girls who are carried away by the excitement. . . . From these cribs, and the many big houses, is the deriving source of the monster's great wealth—he who has paid the police and influenced politicians in his behalf for years. His monthly income from this horrible traffic is several

thousands of dollars. He has become very wealthy from the pitiful earnings of human beings in debauchery.

As prostitute or as madam, Josie's years in the trade were filled with degradation and deception. "If one is to be successful financially, they must assume a variety of distasteful roles—lover, confidant, and entertainer," Josie admitted. Big money customers were made to feel like they were the house's favorite clients. In truth these men were considered worthless. "We haven't any regard for him in our hearts," Josie wrote, "knowing that he has left a loving and truthful wife at home, who is counting the minutes of his absence."

Public women were considered outcasts by churches, and hospitals turned them away when they came searching for healthcare. "Our women have absolutely no friends outside of their world," Josie lamented in her journals. "No flood of pity will rush into the souls of good people for our benefit." She was appalled that laws were in place to prohibit the abuse of dogs, but there were no laws at all to protect and care for so-called sporting women.

Josie Washburn retired in 1907 and found legitimate work managing a boarding house. Hoping to educate people about the misery associated with the life of a public woman and the exploitation of prostitutes by ruthless businessmen and government officials, she began writing a book. Using the journal entries and notes she had penned over her twenty-seven years in the business, she created a manuscript that described the horrible conditions inherent in a life of prostitution. She blamed corrupt men for the continuation of the profession and noted that no matter what they might say, they would never abolish it:

As long as men desire the services found at parlor houses there will be men who solicit women for such services. Too many men derive wealth and political influence from prostitution to willingly end it.

Josie Washburn's attempts to bring about change in the trade went beyond authoring a book. In 1911, she asked the Nebraska legislature for funds to build a home for prostitutes who wanted to leave the business. Her request of $100,000 was denied. Josie likely could have predicted as much; in her 1907 journal she wrote:

That the underworld woman is not permitted to reform is the firm conviction of all of our people.

This conclusion is forced upon us by the decision of the Christian world, which is that if a woman has fallen, she will never reform, and there is no use to try to help her.

If the men, young or old, who come to us in our castles, houses, cribs, or dives, and associate with us in the sin of the underworld, should be disgraced and branded by the Christian and business world, this would go a long way toward reformation, as the men would try to avoid the disgrace.

Does the Christian man or woman refuse to associate on equal terms with a man who is our associate and supplies the money which keeps your institutions going?

Not long after Josie was denied the capital for her project, she relocated to Minneapolis and concentrated her efforts on getting her book published, but the subject matter of her book made it impossible to find a publisher. The male-dominated industry took offense at her claim that the root of prostitution could be traced to men.

Rejection from mainstream publishers only made Josie more determined to see her work in print. In 1925, she invested her own money and published the book, *The Underworld Sewer*, herself. She dedicated the work to the people of "Village, City, State, and Nation, which both consciously and unconsciously maintain the social evil."

Three years after the book was released, Josie moved to Spokane, Washington, and virtually disappeared from the annals of history. Historians speculate that she changed her name and started a new life, putting to rest her tainted past forever.

KATE HORONY

THE HUNGARIAN MADAM

*It's laughable how some people will talk. I laugh at how
often I turn up dead and buried.*
—Big Nose Kate, 1883

Kate Horony removed the crystal stopper from a glass container filled
with brandy and poured herself a drink. The svelte, well-dressed nineteen-
year-old took a big gulp, and then poured another. She slammed the
brandy back and trained the derringer in her right hand on a man's body
that was stretched out before her. Jonas Stonebreak was lying in a pool
of blood, with a bullet in his upper torso. He stirred a bit, struggling to
lift his head off the floor. He glanced around the bedroom at the
Tribolet parlor house until his blurry eyes came to rest on Kate.

She stared down at him, her eyes filled with contempt. The lifeless
frame of Madam Blance Tribolet was slumped in a chair next to Jonas.
Kate motioned to the dead woman with her empty glass. "You had no
cause to kill Blance," she told him. "You're a miserable cur." She blinked
away a tear and poured another drink, while Jonas tried to sit up.

"She was asking for it," he offered, spitting blood.

"No she wasn't," Kate responded, pointing the gun at his head.
"But you sure as hell have." She squeezed the trigger, firing off a shot
that lodged a bullet in Jonas's forehead. He collapsed in a heap. Kate
drank down another brandy before pocketing her gun and leaving the
room.

Blance Tribolet was the first madam Kate Horony, better known as Big Nose Kate, ever worked for. She was more than an employer to the young woman; she was a friend and surrogate mother as well. The revenge Kate sought for the murder of her benefactress was one of many defining moments in the life of one of the West's most notorious prostitutes.

Kate was born on November 7, 1850, in Budapest, Hungary, and named Mary Katherine Horony. Orphaned at the age of fifteen, Kate and her four siblings went to live with their guardian, Otto Schmidt, in Davenport, Iowa. Schmidt was a farmer who instantly put the Horony children to work on his property. He was a strict taskmaster who physically abused the Horonys and attempted to rape Kate. She managed to escape his attack, hitting him in the head with an ax handle and rendering him unconscious. Fearing for her life, Kate ran away. She ended up at the banks of the Mississippi. She had no money and, with the exception of her curvaceous figure and sharp mind, no prospects.

The river docks were crowded with boat crews, fur trappers, and gamblers—all of whom might take advantage of Kate if given the chance. She managed to avoid their persistent come-ons and sneak aboard the steamship, *Ulysses.* "Burlington" Fisher, the vessel's captain, found the teenager and questioned her about why she was there.

The trapped orphan made up numerous stories about her situation before finally confessing the truth about the death of her parents. She told the captain that she was trying to get to a nun's convent in St. Louis. Fisher agreed to transport Kate to her destination and keep her safe during the trip. The voyage had barely begun, however, when the pair became lovers. Once the ship arrived in St. Louis, Captain Fisher helped place Kate in the Ursuline Convent.

Living in a convent was not ideal for the strong-willed Kate, and in a matter of days she ran away. While on the run this time, she met and fell in love with Silas Melvin. The two married, settled in Missouri, and eventually had a son. Less than a year after his birth, however, a cholera epidemic claimed the lives of both Kate's husband and her child.

Devastated and alone, on the streets and penniless, Kate found a home at Blance Tribolet's parlor house. Madam Tribolet introduced the young woman to the lucrative prostitution trade. With Blance's instruction Kate became one of the house's busiest ladies.

The lifestyle suited Kate. She kept herself adorned in the finest fashions and carried herself with an air of class that the other women of the house seemed to lack. Historians have suggested that her inviting Hungarian accent enticed a fair number of men to seek out her company. Madam Tribolet doted over her protégé and helped guide her career.

After avenging the death of her mentor, Kate wandered about the cow towns of Missouri and Kansas. In 1874, she settled in Wichita and went to work at a parlor house owned and operated by Wyatt Earp's sister-in-law, Bessie. Kate claims to have had an affair with the famed lawman, but there is no historical proof to support that assertion. Letters written between Kate and her niece alleged that Wyatt made frequent calls on the "soiled dove" while she worked at Bessie's house. Kate wrote that Wyatt eventually ceased calling on Kate and reunited with his common-law wife, Mattie Blaylock.

Kate Horony left Wichita in 1875 and headed to Dodge City. News of the money to be made by public women in Fort Griffin, Texas, then drove her south. Fort Griffin was a popular settlement filled with cowboys, buffalo hunters, and outlaws. Doc Holliday was one of the outlaws who frequented the boomtown outside of the Army post. Kate was smitten the moment she met the legendary figure.

John Henry Holliday had blonde hair, a neatly trimmed moustache, and pale blue eyes. He had an air of sophistication about him and a devil-may-care attitude that drew Kate to him. He despised "sporting girls" with light-colored hair, painted faces, and exposed legs. Kate's dark features, voluptuous form, and determined nose—which prompted colleagues and clients to refer to her as "Big Nose Kate"—better suited the outlaw. Doc was also attracted to Kate's fiery temper, fiercely independent nature, and marvelous vocabulary of curse words. Doc and Kate shared many of the same qualities, and the combination of their strong personality traits made for a rocky relationship.

By the time their paths crossed, Doc had made a name for himself as "the gambler dentist with the fast gun." Kate was star-struck and made herself available to the gambler dentist at any time of the night or day. When Doc wasn't with her, Kate would search the gambling halls and watering holes in the area, looking for him. She was not satisfied with their occasional rendezvous. Doc was suffering from advanced tuberculosis, and Kate was determined to make him see that she was good medicine for him. She eventually wore him down and became a permanent fixture in his tumultuous life.

No matter who her full-time lover was, Big Nose Kate never relied on anyone for financial support. She was a self-sufficient woman who worked in parlor houses or ran her own brothel to earn a living. Doc Holliday was indeed the one man she truly loved, but he did not pay her way.

Any questions Doc might have had about Kate's devotion to him were answered one evening, after a poker game turned deadly. Doc had shoved a knife into the chest of a fellow card player he had caught cheating. The Fort Griffin sheriff arrested Holliday and took him away to a makeshift jail at a local hotel. Kate helped Doc escape by setting fire to the building. While the authorities were preoccupied with the blaze, Kate rescued her paramour from the hangman's noose.

After Doc and Kate fled from the burning Texas hotel, they headed for Dodge City, Kansas. Once there, Doc set up a dental practice, and the two moved into Deacon Cox's Boarding House, registered as "Mr. and Mrs. J.H. Holliday." Despite their registration as man and wife, Kate and Doc were never legally married.

Doc played nightly card games with his new friends, Wyatt Earp and Bat Masterson. He began to spend less and less time with his dentistry practice, and his late-night drinking brought on long bouts of sickness. Kate would stay by his side and help him get well. He loved her for it, but he also resented her good health. They fought constantly, and even though they lived as common-law husband and wife, Kate continued to work as a prostitute. Her job influenced Doc's view of her, and he oftentimes treated her as inferior. Kate, however, wouldn't quit. She liked her occupation because it provided her with her own income and she didn't have to answer to anybody.

Kate managed to make herself indispensable to Doc. She knew how to ease him through his coughing attacks, and he actually enjoyed the volatile relationship they shared. He liked her coarseness and vulgarity. Wyatt Earp was witness to many of their fights, and on several occasions he suggested to Doc that he should "belt her one." Doc would reply, "Man cannot do what he wants to in this world, but only that which will benefit him."

From Dodge City, the couple moved to Colorado, then on to Las Vegas, New Mexico. Doc continued to work as a dentist during the day and run a saloon at night. Kate plied her trade at a dance hall in nearby Sante Fe. In 1879, Wyatt Earp rode into town on his way to Arizona and convinced Doc to go along with him. Kate was furious with Wyatt's interference in their relationship. She tried to talk Doc out of going, but his dedication to the Earps proved to be stronger then any hold that Kate had on him.

Doc joined the Earps in Tombstone in 1880, without Kate. She moved to Globe and bought a hotel with the money she had made running a parlor house in Sante Fe. By March of 1881, Kate decided she couldn't live without Doc and headed off to Tombstone. During their time apart, Doc had grown more pale and thin. His bright eyes had faded to a cold, hard gray, and his head was topped by enough white hairs to make his hair appear ash-blonde. It wasn't long after they were reunited that their romance showed signs of the usual strain. Kate was jealous of the time he spent with the Earps and never failed to make her feelings known.

On the night of March 15, 1881, armed robbers attempted to hold up a stage near the town of Contention, Arizona. In the holdup attempt, the robbers killed the driver and a passenger. An angry, drunken Kate later told Cochise County Sheriff Behan and his deputy, Frank Stillwell, that Doc was responsible for the robbery and murders, and she signed an affidavit to that effect.

When Kate was sober and realized what she had done, she repudiated the statement, and the judge dropped the charges. An angry Doc gave Kate some money and a stagecoach ticket and sent her back to Globe. But she wasn't gone for good. She would return to Tombstone one more time to see her beloved Doc. She was on hand to witness the gunfight at the OK Corral from her room at Fly's Boarding House. Once the smoke cleared, she again went back to Globe and the thriving bordello she owned there.

In 1887, Kate received word that Doc was near death and traveled to Colorado to be with him. Historical records indicate that she took him to her brother's ranch near Glenwood Springs.

Doc died in a Glenwood Springs hotel on November 8, 1887. The following year Kate married George Cummings, a blacksmith. But shortly after exchanging vows, Kate left her new husband. It seems Cummings lacked the passion and ability to spar with her that Doc had possessed. He later committed suicide.

Kate moved into the Arizona Pioneers' Home in 1935. She passed away five years later, on the second of November. The inscription on her tombstone does not list the many names she used at various times in her career as a madam and prostitute. Nor does it contain a verse or statement about her adventurous life. It simply reads, "Mary K. Cummings."

MATTIE SILKS

DENVER'S RED LIGHT QUEEN

I went into the sporting life for business reasons and for no other. It was a way for a woman in those days to make money, and I made it. I considered myself then and I do now—as a business woman. I operated the best house in town and I had as my clients the most important men in the West.

—Mattie Silks, 1926

Mattie Silks made her way through the crowd assembled at the Lucky Chance Saloon and headed toward a wooden staircase that led to a bank of occupied rooms. Every cowhand in Colorado seemed to be drinking and gambling at the popular Denver establishment. A piano player pounded out a standard on an out-of-tune upright. Several men jumped to their feet, grabbing any woman within reach and twirling them around. The laughing, drunken dancers paid no attention to Mattie as she pushed past them, and she was equally oblivious to them.

The stairs groaned under her heavyset form, and she stumbled a bit over her long, billowing skirt before lifting the fabric to her ankles. Her attractive, round face was streaked with tears, and her eyes were stern and focused. She fingered the ivory-handled pistol in the hidden pocket of her outfit, making sure the weapon was ready for quick use.

She paused at the top of the landing and gazed down the long corridor. A cacophony of sounds emanated from behind the closed doors on either side of the hall. She stopped in front of the first door and listened.

She did the same at the second door. Standing outside the third door, she listened as a man's familiar voice spoke softly to a woman, who responded with a playful giggle.

Mattie's hand reached for the doorknob and stopped. The urge to burst into the room was overwhelming, and for a moment she fought to curb her fury. But the muffled sound of two people in the throes of passion persuaded her to throw open the door and pull out her gun.

Cortez Thomson, a tall, lean, sandy-haired Texan with a handlebar moustache, looked up at the intruder. Lillie Dab, the rumpled, red-headed woman under him, did the same. A long, awkward silence passed between the three. More out of nervousness than anything else, Cort began to laugh. Lillie followed suit and soon the pair were in stitches over the scene. Mattie's blue eyes burned with rage. She aimed her gun at Lillie and squeezed the trigger. Lillie screamed and grabbed her head. Horrified, Lillie glanced down at the sheet, expecting to see blood. Instead she saw two of her long curls on the bed beside her. The shot had missed her body and clipped off her hair.

Cort jumped up and scrambled for his holster and gun, which were draped across the frame of the bed. Mattie turned her weapon in his direction and fired a shot into the floorboard next to his feet. Lillie screamed again, and Cort quickly decided against going for his gun. When Mattie shot at the headboard, Lillie rolled out of bed and quickly crawled toward the door. Mattie cocked the gun yet again and leveled it at the naked woman. Another round went off into the floor, barely missing Lillie. Cort managed to retrieve his weapon and hit Mattie over the head with the butt of his gun. She fell in a heap beside the scuffed wood, which was now splintered with bullet holes.

Mattie Silks, the Queen of Denver's Red Light District, was involved in more than one violent altercation over her lover, Cort Thomson. Her fearless attempts to hold onto her man by any means possible made her one of the most renowned madams in the West.

Born in 1847 on a small farm in Kansas, Mattie was a vivacious child with massive potential. By her mid-teens she was a curvaceous brunette, with sultry blue eyes and a head for business. By the time she was eighteen years old, she had worked as a public woman in Abilene and Dodge City. At nineteen she was managing a profitable parlor house in Springfield, Illinois.

Historians can only speculate how Mattie acquired her handle. Some suggest she took the name Silks from a man she once knew in Kansas. Others claim her love of silk material prompted clients to refer to her as Madam Silks.

After hearing that thousands of men were moving into the boom-towns and cow towns of Colorado, Mattie decided to purchase a parlor house in Georgetown, which was known as the "Silver Queen of the Rockies." Twenty-three thousand dollars a year in silver were being pulled out of the hills in the area in the early 1870s. Mattie's brothel collected a large portion of those riches.

The employees at Mattie Silks's house were considered to be the "fairest frails in town." She was particular about the women she hired and required them to meet certain standards. "I never took a girl into my house who had had no previous experience of life and men," she said. "That was a rule of mine. . . . No innocent, young girl was ever hired by me. Those with experience came to me for the same reasons that I hired them. Because there was money in it for all of us."

An evening of pleasure with one of her ladies could cost anywhere from $10 to $200. Madam Silks claimed 40 percent of that income for herself. In exchange she provided her staff with comfortable rooms, meals, and laundry service. By 1875 Mattie was one of the wealthiest businesswomen in the trade.

Mattie's charm and success attracted numerous men, but she shunned many of their advances. It wasn't until she met Cortez D. Thomson that she decided to share her life with another. Cort was unlike the other men who had called on her. He was not a miner or a cowboy, but a foot runner. Lithe and agile, he raced challengers for large sums of money. The flamboyant racer wore pink tights and star-spangled trunks when he ran, and gamblers and the curious would turn out in droves to watch him compete. Mattie was captivated by Cort's good looks and confident air. He was drawn to her charm and her money. Ignoring the fact that Cort was married and had a child in Texas, Mattie entered into a relationship with him. In 1876, Madam Silks relocated to Denver. The prospect of making even more money enticed her to the growing town. Cort naturally followed.

Mattie's fashionable Denver brothel was a three-story brick mansion with twenty-seven rooms. It was nicely decorated and well furnished. Clients were greeted by the home's owner at a magnificent, wooden front door. They were then escorted into the main parlor and serenaded by an orchestra. It was there that they had a chance to become acquainted with the beautiful and elegantly dressed boarders. Mattie kept the names of her regular customers on a list. "I never showed that list to anyone," she told a newspaper reporter in 1926. "If a man did not conduct himself as a gentlemen, he was not welcome nor ever permitted to come again. And his name was removed from the list."

Madam Silks's parlor house was one of the most expensive brothels in Denver. Mattie's weekly income was staggering, and Cort quickly grew accustomed to an extravagant lifestyle. He and Mattie enjoyed the finest foods and wines, and purchased tailor-made clothes from Paris. Cort spent a great deal of Mattie's wealth betting on horse races. He generally lost more than he won. On those rare occasions when he did win, he made small purchases for Mattie. One such item was a diamond-encrusted cross. She wore the cross on a long chain around her neck, and it became her trademark.

Historians estimate that Cort spent or gambled away more than $75,000 of Mattie's money. In addition to squandering her finances, he betrayed her with other women. The most notable was with a rival madam named Kate Fulton.

Cort's relationship with the lovely and tempestuous Kate had been a simple dalliance to him, but she perceived it as much more. Kate vigorously pursued Cort and desperately tried to convince him to leave Mattie. Mattie knew about the affair and for the most part was able to overlook Cort's indiscretion. On August 24, 1877, however, she was forced to deal with the persistent Madam Fulton once and for all.

Mattie and Cort hosted a grand celebration at the posh Olympic Gardens to announce their engagement. Kate maneuvered her way into the party and accused Mattie of "stealing her man." The pair's verbal sparring escalated into a gunfight.

Anxious guests and townspeople lined Denver's Colfax Avenue to watch the women settle their differences with pistols. Mattie and Kate stood back to back, pistols at the ready. After pacing off a short distance, they turned and fired on one another. When the smoke cleared, the only person down was Cort.

Both Mattie's and Kate's bullets had missed their mark, but one of Kate's rounds had hit Cort in the neck. Mattie hurried to her lover's side and stemmed the flow of blood from the flesh wound with a lace handkerchief. She then escorted Cort to the hospital. Law enforcement officials took Kate to jail in restraints. Local newspapers referred to the incident as "a disgraceful occurrence of the fast element."

In a short time Cort was back on his feet. Madam Silks whisked her lover off to Kansas City for a much-needed break from the routine. She showered him with gifts and clothing, and indulged herself in the finer things as well. The pair spent a great deal of time at the Overland Park racetrack, and Mattie became so enamored with the sport that she invested in a racing stable. With the exception of a chestnut gelding named Jim Blaine, all of her horses were losers.

In 1884, after a seven-year engagement, Mattie and Cort were married. Cort's first wife had died earlier that year, freeing him to make an honest woman out of his long-time lover. For a short time Mattie Silks's life was good. She purchased three other parlor houses in the Denver area, and all of them were extremely successful. Cort's philandering had slowed down a bit. He had, however, developed a costly gambling habit.

With business going as well as it was, and with her marriage as stable as it would ever be, Mattie felt she could now pay more attention to her stable of horses. News that Cort's daughter had died, leaving behind a child of her own, halted any such plans. Cort wanted nothing to do with the orphaned girl and refused to take her in. Mattie did not agree with her husband. She adopted the little girl, named Rita, and placed her in a respected boarding school.

Four years after Mattie assumed responsibility of Rita, Cort passed away. The distraught madam gave her husband a magnificent funeral, spending an untold fortune on the services and his tombstone.

At the age of seventy-seven, after more than four decades working in Colorado's underworld, Mattie remained the leading moneymaker in the profession. As her businesses continued to grow, so did the need to protect her ladies from overzealous clients who might harm the merchandise. With that in mind she hired "Handsome" Jack Ready. Jack was a big, good-looking man who worked not only as Mattie's bouncer, but also as her financial advisor. Their relationship quickly graduated from employer-employee to man and wife. The two married in 1923.

Since the turn of the century, the modern world had ever so slightly been encroaching on Mattie's trade. The Old West ideals of prostitution were tolerated less and less, and government officials were being pushed to abolish the legalization of parlor houses. Police raids on the brothels frightened off customers, and business began to dwindle to nothing. Mattie was forced to shut her doors and sell her homes, including the famed House of Mirrors, which she had purchased from another well-known madam, Jennie Rogers.

Mattie retired to a quiet home just two blocks from one of the five brothels she had once owned. She enjoyed spending time with Jack, her adopted granddaughter, and Rita's children. When Mattie passed away at the age of eighty-two, she willed her estate to her husband and Rita. Over her forty-year career, she had made millions, but when she died, she only had $4,000 in cash, a few pieces of jewelry, and some property.

Madam Silks is buried at the Fairmount Cemetery in Denver, under a headstone that reads simply, "Martha A. Ready, January 7, 1929."

FLORENCE MABEL DEDRICK

OUR SISTER OF THE STREET

*She is heart and soul in the work and has been
wonderfully blessed in her efforts.*
>—Ernest A. Bell, Superintendent of
>Midnight Missions, describing
>Florence Dedrick, 1910

As the Wild West became more civilized, tolerance for prostitution and the women who owned and operated houses of ill fame diminished. Morally upright citizens spoke out against the trade, politicians drafted legislation that made the profession illegal, and missionaries ventured into the parlor houses and cribs to reform the soiled doves.

Sister Florence Mabel Dedrick, a missionary from the Moody Church in Chicago, was dedicated to rescuing women from the "underworld." She believed she had been called by God to "serve her fallen sisters and persuade them to repent." She authored several articles about her experiences in helping to save women from the perils of "evil living." Their salvation was a burden that weighed heavily upon her heart.

In 1910, Sister Florence wrote that she was "more than happy to share her experiences with readers everywhere." The following excerpt is from a publication entitled "For God's Sake Do Something":

What are we doing for our tempted sisters? Are we going to let the business of prostitution have free and undisputed sway without a word of protest, blighting and ruining the homes in this fair land of liberty and freedom? Are we going to let evil exist and triumph and not rise up in arms against it?

The question, what are we doing for our sisters, came up as far back as Solomon's time, but has an answer been found? No! It was only when Jesus met the woman at the well did a new life open for our unfortunate sisters. I plead with you do not draw away your skirts for fear of contamination. Remember, the Master Himself allowed a fallen woman to wash His feet with her tears and wipe them with the hairs of her head. It was a fallen woman who was first to see the omissions and deficiencies of hospitality forgotten by others. Are not fallen women included within the scope of the Master's great commission?

A woman may fall lower than a man, but this is due to her sensitive moral nature. With the conviction that she is past redemption, doors closed, no one loving her, people, yes, her own sex, ostracizing her—she becomes hopeless, desperate, reckless. Can you blame her? Again, let me recall to your mind, Jesus Himself forgave and renewed repentant ones. Even when a woman had fallen to the depths of sin and degradation He still called her "woman."

Not every girl who leads a life of sin and shame is by any means a free person. They are in a sense a slave to sin and God is no respecter of persons and the same judgment will be hers unless she hastens home to her Father's House, where room and to spare and warm welcome awaits her. Not many doors await in her world.

An example of this is found in the case of a young girl in Colorado who, ruined, went from door to door to find someone who would befriend her. Some have one excuse, some another. All said: "We cannot take you in." Tired, discouraged, only one door open, and that is the brothel door from whence she once came.

Many ask: "Who are these girls who go astray?"—having an idea that it is only the ignorant class who are down in sin. It is not so, and let me undeceive everyone on this point, though many, many of the ignorant class do go astray also. Satan is claiming our best, our VERY best girls of education, refinement, advantages and religious training. In one of the most notorious and elegant resorts, known in the red light district of Texas, there are college girls, who have had every advantage. Only lately, as I have done personal work there, did I learn that these very girls were at times in such despair as to threaten to commit suicide.

Some girls come to me when in these resorts and say: "I used to sing in Moody Church Choir." Others will tell you they went through every department of the Sunday school, some were Sunday school teachers. Members of almost every Church you will find among them. When these facts are considered one cannot help but realize the need for action.

A sad incident occurred in one of Colorado's churches. Seven or eight boys, whom everyone considered pure, were found, upon investigation, to have caused the ruin of thirteen girls. One girl, in telling me how she had been led astray said she had been getting $3.50 a week for her lifestyle.

When it comes to reform there must be cooperation on the part of the state, the home, and the church. What we need is a practical salvation, something more than saying: "Be ye saved." The church can do what the state cannot, and vice versa. Not only present, but future generations are in danger. Vice and crime are being flaunted, as it were, and advertised in our very faces. Every man, woman, and child has a place in the battle.

It is girls whose ages are from thirteen to twenty-two who are going astray, even as young as nine years; deceived, betrayed, led away by the promise of making a fortune selling themselves. The conscience of these girls is by no means dead. Upon giving one my card, she said: "If I had only known it before; many tell me about being a Christian, and another world, but I never could understand it." The cry of another sinsick girl was, amid sobs and tears: "Oh! It is awful and sin has done it!"

Oh, Christian women, mothers, give recognition to the fact; yes, welcome it, that a fallen woman can be saved, and extend to her sympathy, encouragement and love! Especially let me say: "The girls of today are the mothers of the morrow, and as in the life and influence of mother rests the making of men and nations, let us, with God's help, save the girls." Knowing the price of a single soul, the burden of my heart is, that the minds of our American people may be so stirred and awakened to the existing causes of evils that are engulfing our girls, that we will each take our part, appoint ourselves as a committee of one, to do all we can to stamp out this monstrous soul scourge, and hinder and stop its further progress.

TESSIE WALL

BARBARY COAST MADAM

Drink that up, boys! Have a drink on Tessie Wall!
—Madam Tessie Wall's invitation to
officers at the Policeman's Ball,
after laying a $1,000 bill on the bar, 1913

A parade of horse-drawn carriages deposited fashionably dressed San Francisco citizens at the entrance of the Tivoli Theatre. A handsome couple emerged from one of the vehicles, holding hands. Across the street, hidden in the shadows of an alleyway, a lone woman eyed the pair intently. Once the couple entered the building, Tessie Wall stepped out of the darkness and into the subdued light from a row of gas lamps that lined the busy thoroughfare. Tears streamed down the svelte blonde's face. The pain of seeing the man she loved with another woman was unbearable.

Several hours earlier, Tessie and her ex-husband, Frank Daroux, had entertained passersby with a robust argument over the other woman in his life. After accusing Frank of being a liar and a thief, Tessie begged him for another chance and promised to make him forget anyone else he was involved with. Frank angrily warned Tessie that if she started anything, he would put her "so far away that no one would find her."

The words he had said to her played over and over again in her head. "You've got my husband," she mumbled to herself. "And you'll get yours someday. It's not right." She choked back a torrent of tears, reached into her handbag, and removed a silver-plated revolver. Hiding the weapon in the folds of her dress, she stepped back into the dark alleyway and waited.

It wasn't long before Frank walked out of the theatre, alone. Standing on the steps of the building, he lit up a cigar and cast a glance into the night sky. Preoccupied with the view of the stars, Frank did not see Tessie hurry across the street toward him. Before he realized what was happening, Tessie pointed the gun at his chest and fired. As Frank fell backwards, he grabbed hold of the rim of a nearby stage. Tessie unloaded two more shots into his upper body, and Frank collapsed in a bloody heap.

Tessie stood over his nearly lifeless frame, sobbing. When the police arrived, she was kneeling beside Frank, the gun still clutched in her hand. When asked why she had opened fire on him, she wailed, "I shot him because I love him, God-damn him!"

Tessie Wall was one of the Barbary Coast's most popular madams. From the moment she entered the business in 1898, her life had been mired in controversy. Born on May 26, 1869, she was one of ten children. Her mother, who died at age forty-four, named her chubby, ash-blonde daughter Teresa Susan Donahue. Her father, Eugene, was a dockworker and spent a considerable amount of time away from home. Teresa and her brothers and sisters took care of themselves.

By the time she turned thirteen, Teresa—or Tessie, as she was called by friends and family—had developed into a beautiful, curvaceous young woman. She turned heads everywhere she went in the Mission District where she lived.

In 1884, Tessie accepted a marriage proposal from Edward M. Wall, a handsome fireman who was twice her age. Edward was a heavy drinker and was often out of work because of his "weakness." Tessie supported both of them with her job as a housekeeper. Two years after the pair married, they had a son. Joseph Lawrence Wall's life was short, however. He died four months after his birth, from respiratory complications. Tessie was devastated and, following her husband's example, took up drinking to dull the pain.

Joseph's death also had an adverse effect on Edward and Tessie's relationship. Both blamed the other for the loss. The Walls' marriage ended in bitter divorce.

Historians believe that heartbreak over her child's death and the subsequent demise of her marriage contributed to Tessie's decision to enter into a life of prostitution.

Before venturing out on her own, Tessie continued to keep house for some of San Francisco's most prominent citizens. While in their employ, Tessie learned about the unconventional desires and habits many of the elite society members possessed. After learning how much money they were willing to pay for their debauchery, she decided to go into business for herself. In 1898, she purchased a brothel and hired a stable of beautiful young ladies to work for her.

In two years' time Tessie's "lodging house" had become so successful that she was able to open a second brothel.

Tessie Wall's bordello was visited by some of the wealthiest businessmen and politicians in the state. Upon entering her business, clients were greeted by elegantly dressed women offering wine and champagne. The home itself was equally inviting and posh. It was furnished with antiques, a large gold fireplace, and plush red-velvet sofas and armchairs. The draperies and bedroom furniture were just as ornate. Tessie had a giant, gold Napoleon bed decorated with swans and cupids. The dresser and matching mirror were gilded, as well.

Madam Wall's parlor house was recognized as one of the best in the city. Tessie herself would spend time with her guests, prior to their departure with a lady of their choosing. She listened intently to their stories about life and work and would laugh uproariously at their jokes. Patrons were so captivated by the charms of their hostess that they often admitted that when they sat down in the parlor and started talking to Tessie, they often forgot what they had come for.

Tessie Wall knew the importance of advertisement. The method she used to promote her house was unconventional, but effective. She would clothe her girls in the latest garments from Paris and New York and send them out on the street for all to admire. Every Saturday afternoon Tessie's girls would hold a parade on Market Street. Everyone in the neighborhood would come out to see the new fashions being worn by the demimonde.

Once other madams saw how popular the parades were, they launched their own exhibitions. It wasn't uncommon on weekends to see numerous women marching on opposite sides of the thoroughfare, modeling the latest styles. Parlor houses with the best showing reaped the benefits in the evening. Due in large part to Tessie's welcoming personality and the voluptuous ladies who worked for her, Tessie's brothel was usually the one that did the most business.

Madam Wall's parlor house yielded a sizeable profit, but the opportunities the income afforded her and the conversation she enjoyed with customers couldn't keep her from thinking about her son. During those melancholy moments she would once again turn to alcohol. By that point in her life, Tessie was able to consume enormous quantities of wine and she could drink most men under the table. She often challenged beer drinkers to champagne-drinking contests. The famous boxer John L. Sullivan was one such participant. Sullivan was unaccustomed to the effects of champagne, and after twenty-one drinks he passed out. Still standing after twenty-two drinks, Tessie won the contest and was forever referred to as "the woman who licked John L. Sullivan."

The life and business Madam Wall had built for herself was almost destroyed by the Great Fire of 1906. A massive earthquake rocked San Francisco on April 18, and subsequently fires broke out in buildings and homes along Market Street. The blaze spread throughout the city, reducing multiple structures to ash.

Despite her best efforts Tessie's parlor house did not survive the inferno. The only item she managed to save was the gold fireplace. When she rebuilt the brothel a year later, the resilient item was put back in place. It became the focal point of the house and the subject of much conversation for years to come.

The new parlor house was just as popular as before, but competition from new rival houses had heightened. Jessie Hayman, the madam from a high-class establishment near Tessie's, had attracted many clients and her business continued to grow daily. Madam Wall was forced to come up with fresh ways to promote her house.

In addition to the weekly parades of her employees dressed in their finest, Tessie decided to show off her staff at music halls and theatres. Every Sunday evening Tessie and her ladies would attend a vaudeville performance at the Orpheum Theatre. She purposely arrived late, so all eyes would be focused on her beauties as they made their way to their seats.

The stunt drastically increased nightly business. When Jessie Hayman learned what Tessie was doing, she too began taking her ladies to the theatre. On Sunday nights the two madams would try and best each other with grand entrances that seemed to upstage the performers. Determined not to be outdone, Tessie decided to keep her girls from attending a couple of shows. The spectacle of their arrival always generated a lot of attention, and she hoped their absence would do the same.

The empty seats did pique the public's interest, and just as the conversation about where they were died down, Tessie and her ladies returned. As the lights dimmed, the curtain went up, the music started, and Madam Wall and her girls made their way down the aisle. As though on cue, the show suddenly stopped, the house lights were turned up again, and all eyes were on Tessie and her ladies.

For every public attempt to increase business, there were private deals being made to do the same. It was not uncommon for hotel clerks, bellboys, headwaiters, chefs at restaurants, and cabbies to be paid handsome sums for directing wealthy men to the finer parlor houses. Such help was generally worth 10 percent of the amount earned from the customer.

Over her long career Tessie made friends with several well-known figures. One such man was politician Milton Latham, who would later become the governor of the state. At the time of their meeting, he was a struggling architect. Tessie was struggling herself. A public outcry against houses like hers had prompted city officials to place restrictions on a madam's ability to add more rooms to her business. Construction on new houses of ill repute was also restricted.

In spite of the limitations, Latham wanted to build Tessie a new bordello. Madam Wall laughed at the thought and reminded him of the police blockade on houses like hers. "It's so strict right now," she told Latham, "that I can't even put out red lights or hang red shades." After Latham managed to convince Tessie that it was doable and that his offer was sincere, she agreed to try and acquire a building permit. To her surprise, she was granted one.

Latham built an exquisite home in the city's Tenderloin District. The three-story, terra-cotta structure had twelve suites, a large kitchen and dining room, a saloon, three parlors, and a ballroom. An average of fourteen women lived and worked at the house. Some came to the ornate business from as far away as France. The majority of Madam Wall's highly sought-after employees were young and blonde. However, a thirty-something brunette, known as Black Gladys, garnered the most attention at the home.

Madam Wall's parlor house at 337 O'Farrell Street was a popular stop for college men and young entrepreneurs. Tessie's clients could pay for the services of her ladies by cash or credit, and they did not normally spend the night. If a gentleman did stay overnight, however, he was sent on his way only after his clothes had been pressed and he had been served a full breakfast.

Among the many repeat customers at Tessie's establishment was Frank Daroux. Frank was a gambler and a politician. He held a high-ranking position within the Republican Party and had a weakness for brothels. One evening in 1909, he wandered into Tessie's place and was instantly captivated by the flamboyant madam. She was equally charmed by him. Frank invited Tessie to dinner, and the two laughed and conversed through an elaborate meal.

The evening left a lasting impression on Frank, not merely because the company was stimulating, but because Tessie drank a considerable amount of wine. In addition to the fine French food the pair was served in a private dining room, Tessie enjoyed twenty bottles of champagne and never left the table.

Tessie was attracted to Frank for a variety of reasons. He resembled Napoleon, a man she thought was devilishly handsome. He was clever, smart, and well respected in the community. It was this kind of respectability that Tessie longed for. After a whirlwind courtship and significant persuasion on her part, the two were married.

Frank felt his career in politics would suffer if it were widely known that he had married a madam, so he insisted the wedding take place out of town and be kept a secret. Tessie reluctantly agreed to his terms, but made him promise that she could host a party to celebrate their commitment to one another. One hundred guests attended the grand affair. They were treated to a delicious feast and eighty cases of champagne.

Frank and Tessie's marriage was rocky from the start. Preoccupied with his public image, Frank demanded that Tessie remove herself as madam and run the business in a more covert manner. Tessie agreed, hoping the action would also allow her to spend more time with her husband. Frank, however, often left his new wife alone while he oversaw activities at various gambling houses he owned. When he was home, neighbors would overhear the pair loudly arguing in the early hours of the morning.

The difficulties between the two worsened when a new mayor and city council, bent on reform, were elected to office. The conservative public servants wanted to stamp out gambling and prostitution in San Francisco. Once Tessie's and Frank's livelihoods were threatened, they turned on one another.

In an effort to convince politicians that his business practices and personal life were respectable, Frank removed himself even further from his bride. He befriended the newly elected officials, convincing them that profits earned from his establishment could financially benefit themselves and the city. He attended posh social engagements and rallies, unaccompanied by Madam Wall.

The more powerful Frank became politically, the more he tried to persuade Tessie to sell the parlor house. He reasoned that if she got out of the business, it would ultimately make him look better once news of their marriage became common knowledge. As further enticement to give up the parlor house, Frank purchased a home for Tessie in the country. The gesture did not bring about the desired result. Tessie refused to leave the bustle of the city. "I'd rather be an electric light pole on Powell Street," she told her husband, "than own all the land in the sticks."

No matter how much she might have questioned the wisdom of marrying a man who did not accept her as she was, Tessie's dreams of being embraced socially by San Francisco's elite never wavered. She longed to be invited to chic affairs where important and well-respected guests appeared.

By the spring of 1911, she had managed to wrangle an invitation to the Greenway Cotillion, a dinner and dance held to honor the city's founding fathers. The invitation, for Madam Wall and twelve of her girls, was procured by a politician and regular guest of the parlor house and came with a stipulation. If the ladies chose to attend, their identities had to be disguised by champagne-bottle costumes they were required to wear. Tessie agreed.

Her appearance at the cotillion, even if it was disguised, impelled an unnamed socialite to invite Madam Wall to the annual Mardi Gras Ball. Wearing tails and a top hat, Frank attended the gala with his wife. Tessie's dress was tasteful and understated. She was disappointed, but not surprised, that her name was not listed in the local newspaper as one of the Mardi Gras attendees. She remedied the omission by reporting the loss of an expensive diamond brooch at the ball. The report was followed by a lost-and-found article placed in the *San Francisco Examiner.* Everyone who read the newspaper that day knew the notorious O'Farrell Street madam had been at the Mardi Gras Ball.

Having managed to get herself on the guest list for many more engagements, Tessie was able to convince Frank that she was no longer political poison and was now worthy of a church wedding. Frank consented to a public ceremony, but was adamant about Tessie retiring from the business.

This time she acquiesced and transferred the management of the house to one of her employees. Given the magnitude of the sacrifice, Tessie expected Frank to do something for her in return. At her request, he promised to make all the arrangements for the reception and agreed to her guest list, choice of music, and location.

Once they secured a priest to marry them, a wedding date was set. Nearly two years from the date Frank and Tessie were initially married, the two renewed their vows. The second ceremony was held in the rectory of St. Mary's Cathedral.

Within hours of the nuptials, the Darouxs were exchanging insults. Frank had disregarded all of Tessie's requests for the reception, and she verbalized her irritation in a toast, during which she announced that she was returning to her parlor house business as quickly as she could. Toward the end of the evening, the pair had once again reconciled. Frank took that opportunity of brief calm to present his wife with a wedding gift. The July 12, 1911, edition of the *San Francisco Chronicle* reported on his expensive gesture of affection, with a headline that read, "$10,000 Pearl Necklace Wedding Gift to Bride/Frank Daroux Marries Miss Theresa Donahue."

After a brief honeymoon, Frank and Tessie returned to the lives they had made for themselves. Frank kept active in politics and oversaw business at his gambling dens. Tessie focused on her brothel.

When religious groups staunchly opposed to parlor houses began a crusade to drive them out of business, Madam Wall's place was a prime target. Frank did nothing to stop the powers-that-be from threatening her livelihood. But that was the least of her problems. Unbeknownst to Tessie, her husband was betraying her in a more profound way.

Frank and Tessie's relationship had always been a volatile one. They never shied away from quarreling in public. Frank grew tired of the embarrassing outbursts and was frustrated with the way it diminished his influence with key political figures. His attention eventually turned to a less combative woman he met at a fundraiser. In 1915, the two began having an affair. Tessie found out and vowed to kill the woman if she came near her husband again. Frank stayed in the marriage another two years before walking out on Tessie and filing for divorce.

Like all of the other disagreements Tessie and Frank had in their eight years of marriage, the fight over how their union would end was made public as well. Tessie made it clear to all who would listen that she did not want to lose Frank, and she contested the divorce numerous times. After a long and vicious court battle, the marriage was finally dissolved.

Tessie returned to her house to nurse her wounds. Her heart was broken. She couldn't accept that Frank was officially out of her life. In a desperate attempt to win him back, she secretly followed him around, waiting for a chance to speak with him and convince him to return to her.

The evening Frank was shot, the two had quarreled over Tessie's threat to appeal the divorce. Frank warned his ex-wife that he'd "break her" if she went through with the action. He hurled a string of obscenities at her as he turned and walked away. She heard from a friend that Frank and his mistress were going to the theatre that evening, and she decided to confront the two there.

"Then I didn't know what I did," Tessie explained to the police after the shooting. When asked about the gun, Tessie told authorities that she bought it because of the other woman. "That woman took my husband away from me," she cried. "For three or four years she has been going with him. It made me mad." Tessie pleaded with police to take her to the hospital where Frank was so she could see him. As they transported the sobbing madam to the sanitarium, she professed her undying love for her "darling husband."

Frank was conscious when Tessie entered the emergency room. The three bullets she had emptied into his upper torso had missed his vital organs. Doctors expected him to make a full recovery. The police escorted Tessie to his bedside and asked Frank if she was the one who shot him. "Yes, she shot me," he responded. "Take her away. I don't want to see her." According to the *San Francisco Chronicle,* "Tessie Daroux lifted her handkerchief to her face in a gesture of horror and reeled back into the arms of the officer."

Madam Wall was booked on a charge of intent to kill and held without bail for three months. Bail was finally granted once Frank was given a clean bill of health. In a move that surprised everyone, Frank announced to authorities that he had made a decision not to press charges against Tessie. She took the news as a sign of his continued affection for her and filed an appeal on the divorce. Frank had hoped the incident and his willingness not to prosecute would drive Tessie away. Once he found out that she was appealing the divorce, he changed his mind about pressing charges.

The shooting and subsequent court activity was front-page news. The scandal wreaked havoc on Frank's political future. His peers informed him that he was a liability and they suggested that he relocate. Frank agreed, reversed his decision again about having Tessie prosecuted, and made arrangements to marry his mistress.

Days before Frank was to marry the other woman, Madam Wall again took her gun in her hand. This time she set out to kill her rival. When she found her eating lunch at a popular restaurant, Tessie shot through the glass window at the future Mrs. Daroux. Her aim was poor, however, and the woman was not hit. Tessie was arrested and while she was being held, Frank remarried. With the stipulation that Tessie not be released until they left town, Mr. and Mrs. Daroux agreed not to press charges. Frank and his bride then moved to the East Coast.

Madam Wall went back to her parlor house, boxed up all of the busts and the painting she had of Napoleon, and stored them away. She never fully retired from the trade and remained a controversial figure throughout the duration of her life.

On the morning of April 28, 1932, Tessie pulled an impacted tooth that had been bothering her. That evening, at the age of sixty-three, she died of a hemorrhage following the extraction. Newspapers marked her passing with an obituary that Tessie had preapproved. The *San Francisco Chronicle* wrote:

> One more bit of "the San Francisco that was" has drifted off in that uncharted Sargossa that holds the old Barbary Coast, the Poodle Dog, the Silver Dollar, the Bank Exchange, the Mason Street Tenderloin, and those other gay haunts that made San Francisco famous through the Seven Seas.

LIBBY THOMPSON

DODGE CITY'S SQUIRREL TOOTH ALICE

*"She wasn't a coward; she wasn't a weakling; and she
sure wasn't average."*
—Thelma Thompson Wilson, Squirrel Tooth
Alice's great grand-daughter, 1999

Libby Thompson twirled gracefully around the dance floor of the
Sweetwater Saloon in Sweetwater, Texas. A banjo and piano duo
performed a clumsy rendition of the house favorite, "Sweet Betsy From
Pike." Libby made a valiant effort to match her talent with the mu-
sicians' limited skills. The rough crowd around her was not interested in
the out-of-tune music; their eyes were fixed on the billowing folds of her
flaming red costume. The rowdy men hoped to catch a peek at Libby's
shapely, bare legs underneath the yards of fabric on her skirt, but Libby
was careful to only let them see enough to keep them interested.

Many of the cowboy customers of the Sweetwater were spattered
with alkali dust, grease, or just plain dirt. They stretched their eager,
unkempt hands out to touch Libby as she pranced by, but she managed
to avoid all contact. At the end of the performance she was showered
with applause, cheers, and requests to see more.

That night, Libby was not in an obliging mood. She smiled, bowed
and hurried past the enthusiastic audience as she made her way to the bar
for a drink. A surly bartender served her a glass of apple whisky and she
headed off to the back of the room with her beverage. A large, purple

velvet chair waited for her there in her usual corner spot by the stairs, along with her pets, a pair of prairie dogs. As Libby walked through the mass of people to her thronelike seat, she saw three grimy, bearded men surrounding her seat. One of the inebriated cowhands was poking at her animals with a long stick.

"Boys, I'd thank you kindly to stop that," she warned the unruly trio. The men turned to see who was speaking then broke into a hearty laugh once they saw her. Ignoring the dancer they resumed their harassment of the animals. The animals batted the stick back as it neared them and each time the men would erupt with laughter.

Libby watched the three for a few moments then slowly reached into her drawstring purse and removed a pistol. Pointing the gun at the men she said, "Don't make me ask you again." The drunk cowhands turned to face Libby and she aimed her pistol at the head of the man with the stick. Laughing, the man told her to "go to hell."

"I'm on my way," she responded, pulling the hammer back on the gun. "But I don't mind sending you there first so you can warn them," she added. The cowboy dropped the stick and he and his friends backed away from Libby's chair. One by one they staggered out of the saloon. Libby put the gun back in her purse, scooped up her frightened pets, scratched their heads and kissed them repeatedly.

Known by most as Squirrel Tooth Alice, Libby Thompson was named for a slight imperfection in her teeth and for the burrowing rodents she kept, which were often mistaken for squirrels. Perhaps in spite of, or due to her idiosyncrasies, Alice was one of the most famous madams in the West.

Libby Thompson was born Mary Elizabeth Haley on October 18, 1855 in Belton, Texas. Her parents, James Haley and Mary Raybourne, owned a plantation along the Brazos River. Prior to the Civil War, the Haleys were a wealthy family. Libby and her three brothers and two sisters were accustomed to the finer things in life. When the South lost the War, the Haley fortune went with it. James managed to hold onto his land and his children helped him work the rich soil. He was never a big success as a farmer, but he did manage to keep his family fed. He was not able to protect them from hostile Indian parties that raided homesteads and stole their livestock, however.

In 1864, Comanche Indians raided the Haley plantation and took Libby captive. James and Mary searched for their daughter for three years and finally located the tribe that had taken Libby, offering a ransom for her release. Libby returned home in the winter of 1867.

Thirteen-year-old Libby rarely spoke of her harrowing ordeal among the Comanche—typical of most captives—but speculations as to how the Comanche treated female captives ranged from forcible rape and torture to marriage and servitude. Since Libby showed no physical signs of abuse, her friends and neighbors took that to mean she had willingly submitted to the Indian's demands, and she was shunned from polite society and ostracized from the community.

Rejected by friends, neighbors, and some family members, Libby was driven to keep company with an older man who accepted her in spite of her experience with the Comanche Indians. When Libby brought the gentleman friend home to meet her parents she introduced him as her husband. James was so enraged at the idea of his teenage daughter being taken advantage of he shot and killed Libby's lover, further tarnishing her already questionable reputation.

At the age of fourteen, Libby ran away from home to start life fresh in a new location. She chose Abilene, Kansas, as the spot to begin again, taking a job as a dance-hall girl in one of the town's many wild saloons. It was in one of these establishments that she met a cowboy gambler named Billy Thompson. Billy was ten years older than Libby. He swept her off her feet with his boyish good looks, irresistible charm and promise of an exciting life on the frontier. The two left Abilene together in 1870 and made way for Texas.

When Libby wasn't following her man over the Chisholm Trail while he punched cows for any cattle-drive crew that needed him, the pair was usually holed up in a saloon where Billy would gamble and Libby would dance. Dance hall girls were paid well and could earn even more if they engaged in acts of prostitution, and Libby was not opposed to entertaining gentlemen in that manner if it brought in extra cash. As long as she shared her income with Billy, he didn't object either. The carefree couple drifted from town to town, staying long enough to tire of the place and then move on.

In 1872, Libby and Billy left Texas and headed back to Kansas. This time they settled in Ellsworth. Work was readily available there. Numerous cattle drives came through the area and there was a lot of money to be made and won at the busy saloons. In less than six months Libby and Billie had amassed a small fortune, but most of the pair's wealth was lost after a few luckless nights of gambling. By this time Libby was expecting their first child. Broke and desperate, Billy decided to join a drive heading south as trail boss.

Cohabitation without the benefit of marriage was illegal in the Old West, so Libby and Billy lied about their marital status to get away with living together, but also in order for Libby to go along on the cattle drives. As trail boss, Billy's family was permitted to accompany him. Holed up in the back of a wagon, a pregnant Libby followed the herd from Kansas to Oklahoma. On April 1, 1873, she gave birth to a son and named him Rance. Three months later, in a formal setting, Billy decided to legally marry the mother of his child.

The Thompsons were vagabonds. It was not in their natures to lay down roots, and having a son did not inspire the couple to settle down. They wanted nothing more than to drift freely from cow town to cow town plying their individual trades.

But on August 15, 1873, after an all night drinking spree, a deadly, impulsive act ultimately robbed them of their uninhibited wandering lifestyle, when Billy accidentally shot and killed a Kansas sheriff. He was arrested and the cattle company he worked for bailed him out of jail. Worried about the reprisals from the sheriff's friends and family, fearing for his life and that of his wife and child, Billy and Libby ran. Their itinerant lifestyle then became a matter of necessity rather than choice.

Libby and Billy sought refuge from the law in Dodge City. Libby found work as a dancer, madam, and part-time prostitute. Billy gambled at the saloons around town. They befriended some of the areas most famous residents, including Wyatt Earp and his lover Mattie Blaylock. After Kansas the Thompsons traveled to Colorado and then back to Texas. Along the way, Libby gave birth to three more children, one of whom died from a fever as a child.

By the summer of 1876, Libby and her family were settled in Sweetwater. She and Billy purchased a small ranch outside of town and a dance hall on Main Street. Libby was the main attraction on stage, but the stable of women who worked for her behind the scenes brought in the lion's share of the business. Billy protected his wife whenever he needed to, but spent much of his time away from the saloon, leaving the daily operation of the brothel and tavern to Libby.

Libby was not shy or ashamed of how she earned a living. She openly confessed her profession to anyone who asked. When the census was taken in the area she boldly listed her occupation as "one who diddles and squirms in the dark." Libby's frankness drew customers to her place, but that wasn't the only reason. Her pet "squirrels" also garnered a lot of attention. The "squirrels" or prairie dogs were good pets. She took the small animals with her wherever she went.

Early on in their relationship Billy accepted and encouraged his wife's profession. In later years, however, it was a source of tension between the two. Billy's absence while was on long cattle drives took its toll on the marriage as well. Both began to look to other people to make them happy and fill the voids. Each had a succession of lovers, but they never lost the connection that initially brought them together. They always found their way back to each other. During the course of their twenty-four years of marriage the couple had nine children, though Billy was not present for most of their upbringing, as he continued to travel around the West.

In 1896, Billy returned to Sweetwater after having spent several months in Colorado gambling. During his stay in Cripple Creek, Colorado, he had contracted consumption, and when he arrived in Texas he was dying from the disease. Libby was unable to provide adequate care for her husband so she sent him to his family in southern Texas. Billy passed away on September 6, 1887, at the St. Joseph Infirmary in Houston.

Libby didn't stay single for long. She moved in with a man known to posterity simply as "Mr. Young." Young was a cattle rustler who'd had several run-ins with the law. Historians suspect that Mr. Young, not Billy Thompson, was the father of Libby's ninth child, as she led her deceased husband to believe. If that was the case, Mr. Young proved to be just as bad at parenthood as Billy. Libby was lacking in that department as well. In addition to the nine children she had with Billy, and possibly Mr. Young, she had three more children with two different men. Several of her sons chose a life of crime and many of her daughters followed her into the prostitution trade.

Libby's days as a madam came to an end in 1921. She retired at the age of sixty-six and alternated living with her children. The last month of her life was spent at the Sunbeam Rest Home in Los Angeles. Squirrel Tooth Alice died of natural causes on April 13, 1953. She was ninety-eight years old.

ROSE ELLIS

LAST OF THE OLD WEST MADAMS

There never was a more beautiful person in the world. She lived to help children, filling their Christmas stockings with nickels and dimes, buying gifts and donating Yuletide trees for her girls and the poor.
—Madam Texas Tommy's Chauffeur,
August 11, 1982

The light from a full October moon filtered through the open window beside Rose Ellis's bed. The eighty-four-year-old woman stared thoughtfully into the night sky, then closed her eyes in a half-hearted attempt to block out the peaceful image. Tears rolled off her face onto her pillow. The evening was calm and still, but her emotions were not. The sheets and blankets that once neatly covered her bed were crumpled, and some were lying on the floor. Rose was restless, troubled. "Don't worry," she whispered to herself. "I know what must be done."

San Francisco's Belmont Rest Home, where Rose had just moved, was a sparsely decorated, sterile environment. It was in stark contrast to the parlor houses she had furnished and managed in her younger years. Rose's eighty-two-year-old sister, Buena, was asleep in bed a few feet away. Buena had lived with Rose her entire life and wasn't any more accustomed to her new, homogenized surroundings than Rose was. Somehow, though, Buena had managed to fall asleep. Rose was grateful for that. Buena was developmentally disabled due to a lobotomy that had been performed as a remedy for the shock of her father's death, and she seemed least harassed by the challenges of life when she slept.

As Rose watched her sister's slow and steady breathing, she thought back to the promise she had made her father several years before he passed away: She had pledged to care for her only living relative for the rest of her life.

Old age, lack of funds, and limited options forced Rose to commit herself and Buena to the rest home. Although it was not an ideal situation, Rose was resigned to the living conditions. When doctors informed her that she had very little time to live, she decided to reevaluate the arrangement. The alternative she arrived at was extreme but necessary. It weighed heavily on her heart.

Lifting herself out of bed, Rose shuffled over to a large bureau and slowly opened the top drawer. She removed a .38-caliber, nickel-plated revolver hidden under a stack of camisoles. She opened the gun and loaded two bullets in the chamber. Taking a deep breath she made her way to Buena's bed, knelt down, and kissed her sister on the cheek. Using all the strength in both her aged hands, she pulled the hammer back and held the weapon to her sister's ear. A shot rang out, and Buena was gone.

Tears streamed down Rose's face as she cocked the gun again and pressed it to her own temple. "See you soon, my darling sister," she whispered to Buena's lifeless form. The final shot was fired, and Rose fell in a heap on the floor, the smoking gun still clutched in her hand.

Little is known about Rose Ellis's early life, and what is known was offered to the Searls Historical Library in Nevada City, California, by a worker for the local railroad in Nevada City who had frequently escorted Rose to and from her parlor house and had become a friend.

Rose Aline Ellis was born in 1878. Her father was a wealthy South Dakota miner. Her mother died when Rose and her sister were very young. The girls' father doted on his daughters, giving them every advantage he could afford. In 1910, after learning about business opportunities on the West Coast, he moved his family to San Francisco. He hoped to earn enough to secure a future for his daughters. His death in 1918 shattered Buena, and she was mentally never the same. Doctors performed a lobotomy on the young woman as a remedy for her depression that left her disabled.

Left with the awesome responsibility of caring for her handicapped sister, Rose decided to pursue a career in the oldest profession in the world. Prostitution was a lucrative business. Rose was aware of how well the madams in the area did, and she believed that it was the only job that would bring in the funds needed to help Buena.

Rose managed parlor houses up and down the Bay Area's red-light district from 1918 to 1929. After eleven years of working for various brothel owners, she decided to open her own house in Nevada City, the third largest city in California. The area boasted the richest gold mine in the state, and thousands of ambitious miners had descended on the spot, to extract tons of gold ore from the rich earth.

Rose called her house the Golden Gate Amusement Company. Patrons of the three-story, yellow house on Spring Street referred to the vivacious madam as "Texas Tommy." In order to accommodate three shifts of men working in the mines, she kept her doors open twenty-four hours a day.

Rose used the considerable profits from the house to purchase a grand nightclub that catered to both men and women. It was a fashionable saloon, with sparkling chandeliers, red velvet drapes, a large stage, and an orchestra pit complete with instruments. Champagne flowed from fountains and the finest food was served. Six weeks after the Heidelberg Club opened, the building caught fire and burned to the ground. Arson was suspected, but local authorities could not find the culprit. Nevada County residents speculated that a jealous housewife had torched the brothel, but no proof ever materialized.

Once the ashes had been swept away, Rose's attention shifted solely to her brothel. Her house was always busy, especially on payday— so much so that she had to send for extra entertainers to come in and help. Rose charged clients $2.50 for the company of one of her girls.

Many of the ladies made as much as $50 a night. Rose received 20 percent of their earnings.

Madam Tommy is reported to have been quite generous with the wealth she acquired. Not only did she shower Buena with beautiful clothes and gifts, she also contributed funds to help support poor and hungry children. Whenever a miner died from an on-the-job injury, a wagonload of groceries and firewood would mysteriously appear on the widow's doorstep. Although she never admitted it, townspeople agreed that Texas Tommy was the source of the supplies.

Madam Tommy always appeared in public immaculately dressed. Her auburn-strawberry hair was nicely styled and, more often than not, adorned with a rose. She expected the girls that worked for her to follow her example in keeping a neat and orderly appearance. She believed people treated you with respect if you looked like you respected yourself. On those rare occasions when Rose was treated rudely, she would scold the offender for their actions and warn them to "never let it happen again."

When a teller at the Nevada County bank refused to cash a dividend check that Rose and Buena had received from one of their father's mines in the Dakotas, Rose was so enraged that she stormed out of the establishment, vowing never to do business with them again. She cashed the check instead at an out-of-town bank and used the money to throw a party in every saloon in town. She persuaded all those in attendance to consider ending their association with the Nevada County bank.

Those close to Texas Tommy noted that she was an extravagant spender. It was not uncommon for her to purchase breakfast for her girls and their overnight guests, rent out entire hotels for wild celebrations, buy expensive presents for children in the neighborhood, and treat railroad baggage handlers to a night on the town. Baggage handler Bob Paine recalled a particular night in 1936, when he was witness to Texas Tommy's extreme generosity:

I went to collect the weekly passenger fares. Texas suggested we paint the town a little bit red. She opened a drawer in her office.

I had never seen so much money in my life. $5, $10, and $20 bills to overflowing. On top of the whole pile was a small pearl handled pistol. Texas lifted her satin skirt and stuffed her voluminous bloomers with bills of every denomination and away we went to every saloon in Nevada County.

Madam Tommy's Golden Gate Amusement Company remained in operation until 1942, when the United States Army forced her to close her doors. Off-duty soldiers from a nearby Army post were frequently caught at the parlor house. They were severely reprimanded and told to stay away. Because the country was at war, soldiers were required to wear their uniforms at all times. The order made secret visits to Tommy's place difficult. To get around being spotted entering the bordello, soldiers devised a plan to change into mechanics' overalls and slip in undetected. After a sharp-eyed reporter at the local newspaper exposed the activity, the military and law enforcement moved in and shut the business down.

Madam Tommy and her sister returned to the Bay Area in 1943. Rose took care of Buena as long as she could. Once her health began to decline, she moved them both into a nursing home. On April 26, 1962, news of the tragic demise of the kind-hearted madam and her sister made the front page of the *San Francisco Chronicle:*

She was driven by an undying devotion to her sister . . . Even in death Texas Tommy had class and courage. So let's close this sad story with Jesus' admonishment in his Sermon on the Mount. "Let he who is without sin cast the first stone."

BIBLIOGRAPHY

GENERAL SOURCES

Aikman, Duncan. *Calamity Jane and the Lady Wildcats.* New York: Henry Holt & Company, 1927.

Anonymous. *The Denver Red Book: A Reliable Directory of the Pleasure Resorts of Denver.* Denver, Colorado, 1892.

Ball, Eve. *The Women Who Made the West.* New York: Avon Books, 1980.

Barry, Kathleen. *The Prostitution of Sexuality.* New York: New York University Press, 1995.

Bettmann, Otto. *The Good Old Days: They Were Terrible!* New York: Random House, 1974.

Brown, Dee. *The Gentle Tamers: Women of the Old Wild West.* Lincoln, Nebraska: University of Nebraska Press, 1958.

Churchill, C.M. *The Social Evil.* San Francisco: Bancroft Press, 1872.

Gentry, Curt. *The Madams of San Francisco.* New York: Doubleday & Company, 1964.

Ringdal, Johan and Daly, Richard. *Love For Sale: A World History of Prostitution.* New Haven, Connecticut: Grove Press, 2003.

Seagraves, Anne. *Soiled Doves: Prostitution in the Early West.* Hayden, Idaho: Wesanne Publications, 1994.

JENNIE ROGERS

Bancroft, Caroline. *Six Racy Madams of Colorado*. Boulder, Colorado: Johnson Publishing Company, 1965.

ELEANORA DUMONT

Aikman, Duncan. *Madam Mustache and Other Gaming Ladies*. New York: Henry Holt & Company, 1927.

Drago, Harry S. *Notorious Ladies of the Frontier*. New York: Ballantine Books, 1972.

Ross, Edward A. *Madam Mustache: Pioneer of the Parlor House Circuit*. Cleveland, Ohio: Quirk Books, 1981.

Seagraves, Anne. *Women of the Sierra*. Lakeport, California: Wesanne Enterprises, 1990.

Zauner, Phyllis. *Those Spirited Women of the Early West*. Sonoma, California: Zanel Publications, 1994.

JESSIE HAYMAN

Allen, Robert S. *Jessie Hayman: San Francisco's Other Fire*. New York: Vanguard Press, 1947.

Anonymous. *The Laws of the Town of San Francisco*. San Marino, California: The Huntington Library, 1947.

Caen, Herb. *Only in San Francisco*. New York: Doubleday & Company, 1960.

JESSIE REEVES AND CAD THOMPSON

Hegne, Barbara. *Harlots, Hurdies, & Spirited Women of Virginia City.* Medford, Oregon: FreeStyle Graphics, 2001.

Myres, Sandra L. *Westering Women and the Frontier Experience.* Albuquerque, New Mexico: University of New Mexico Press, 1982.

Selcer, Richard. *Hell's Half Acre.* Fort Worth, Texas: Texas Christian University Press, 1991.

Williams, George. *The Red-Light Ladies of Virginia City, Nevada.* Riverside, California: Tree by the River Publishing, 1984.

JOSIE WASHBURN

Evans, Max. *Madam Millie: Bordellos from Silver City to Ketchikan.* Albuquerque, New Mexico: University of New Mexico Press, 2002.

Walkowitz, Judith. *Prostitution and Victorian Society: Women, Class, and the State.* New York, New York: Cambridge University Press, 1982.

Washburn, Josie. *The Underworld Sewer: A Prostitute Reflects on Life in the Trade, 1871-1909.* Lincoln, Nebraska: University of Nebraska Press, 1925.

KATE HORONY

Boyer, Glenn. "Who Was Big Nose Kate?" *Wyatt Earp: Family, Friends & Foes.* New Mexico: Historical Research Associates, 1997.

Chartier, Joann, and Enss, Chris. *Love Untamed: Romances of the Old West.* Guilford, Connecticut: Globe Pequot Press, 2002.

Coleman, Jane C. *Doc Holliday's Woman*. Clayton, Victoria: Warner Books, 1995.

Fiske, Jack. *Big Nose Kate*. Tombstone, Arizona: Big Nose Kate's Saloon Publishing, 1997.

Jahns, Pat. *The Frontier World of Doc Holliday*. New York: Indian Head Books, 1957.

Robinson, Olivia. *She Did It Her Way*. New York: Putnam Press, 1946.

MATTIE SILKS

Braun, Matt. *Mattie Silks*. Fort Worth, Texas: Pinnacle Books, 1985.

Goldstein, Phil. *The Seamy Side of Denver*. Denver, Colorado: New Social Publishers, 1993.

Miller, Max. *Holladay Street*. New York, New York: New American Library, 1962.

Wallechinsky, David, and Wallace, Irving. *The People's Almanac*. New York: Doubleday, 1975.

FLORENCE MABEL DEDRICK

Bell, Ernest A. *Fighting the Traffic of Young Girls*. Chicago, Illinois: A Cooke County Handbook Series on the White Slave Trade, 1910.

Pivar, David J. *Purity Crusade: Sexual Morality and Social Control*. Westport, Connecticut: Greenwood Press, 1973.

Miller, Ronald Dean. *Shady Ladies of the West*. Tucson, Arizona: Westernlore Press, 1985.

TESSIE WALL

Barnhart, Jacqueline. *The Fair But Frail: Prostitution in San Francisco.* Reno, Nevada: University of Nevada Press, 1986.

Erickson, Bill. *San Francisco Streetwalkers.* San Francisco: Bangkok Publications, 1973.

Wilson, J. Stitt. *The Barbary Coast in a Barbarous Land.* Los Angeles: Socialist Party of California, 1913.

LIBBY THOMPSON

Butler, Anne M. *Daughters of Joy, Sisters of Mercy.* Chicago: University of Illinois Press, 1987.

Gesell, Laurence. *Saddle the Wild Wind: The Saga of Squirrel Tooth Alice and Texas Billy Thompson.* Chandler, Arizona: Coast Aire Publications, 2001.

Rosen, Ruth. *The Lost Sisterhood: Prostitution in America, 1900-1918.* Baltimore, Maryland: The Johns Hopkins University Press, 1983.

ROSE ELLIS

Janicot, Michel. *The Ladies of the Night.* Nevada City, California: Nevada County Historical Society, 1994.

"Texas Tommy—Was She A Saint Or A Sinner?" *The Independent Newspaper,* Nevada City, California, August 11, 1982.

"Whorehouses in the West." *The Independent Newspaper,* Nevada City, California, October 14, 1981.

ABOUT THE AUTHOR

Chris Enss is an award-winning screenwriter who has written for television, short subject films, live performances, and for the movies. She is the author of *Hearts West: True Stories of Mail-Order Brides on the Frontier*, *How the West Was Worn: Bustles and Buckskins on the Wild Frontier*, *Buffalo Gals: Women of Buffalo Bill's Wild West Show*, and *The Doctor Wore Petticoats: Women Physicians of the Old West*. She is also the co-author (with JoAnn Chartier) of *With Great Hope: Women of the California Gold Rush*, *Love Untamed: True Romances Stories of the Old West*, *Gilded Girls: Women Entertainers of the Old West*, and *She Wore A Yellow Ribbon: Women Patriots and Soldiers of the Old West*.

Enss has done everything from stand-up comedy to working as a stunt person at the Old Tucson Movie Studio. She learned the basics of writing for film and television at the University of Arizona, and she is currently working with Return of the Jedi producer Howard Kazanjian on the movie version of *The Cowboy and the Senorita*, their biography of western stars Roy Rogers and Dale Evans. The pair also co-authored *Happy Trails: A Pictorial Celebration of the Life and Times of Roy Rogers and Dale Evans*.

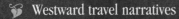